"As through this world I ramble

I see lots of funny men.

Some will rob you with a six-gun

And some with a fountain pen."

- **Woody Guthrie**

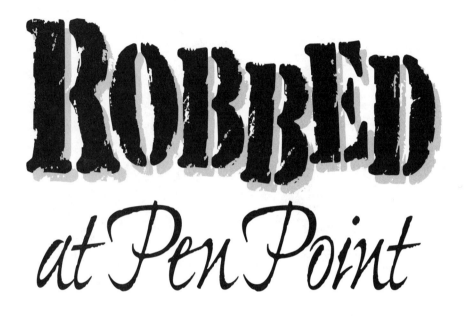

ROBBED
at Pen Point

By Randy Johnston
Professional Malpractice Attorney

Published by
PSG Books   Dallas, Texas

ROBBED at Pen Point
Published by
PSG Books
9603 White Rock Trail, Suite 312
Dallas, Texas 75238
214 340-6223 800 465-1508

ISBN-10   0-9749461-3-3
ISBN-13   978-0974946139

Manufactured in the United States of America
10 9 8 7 6 5 4 3 2 1

Johnston, Randy, 1946-
Robbed at pen point : cheated, lied to and injured by lawyers, doctors, stockbrokers, accountants, financial planners, money managers or business partners? ; prevent it from happening, get even when it does / by Randy Johnston.
p. cm.
ISBN 978-0-9749461-3-9
1. Malpractice--United States. 2. Lawyers--Malpractice--United States. 3. Medical personnel--Malpractice--United States. 4. Commercial crimes--United States. 5. Fraud--United States. I. Title.

KF1289.J64 2008
346.7303'3--dc22
                                        2008040959

*For my family who is always there and for those clients
who've trusted my judgment by allowing me
to help them with their legal problems
over the years.*

Notice

This is a national book that cites cases affected by both federal and state laws. State laws, legal precedents, codes and regulations vary greatly from one jurisdiction to another and change over time. The reader should not use this book for specific legal advice but should seek the advice of those versed in the laws of the jurisdiction where the action is taken.

It must be understood, therefore, that this book provides readers with a general overview related to the issues mentioned, so that they may take legal action or otherwise address these issues better informed.

Reading this book does not establish an attorney-client relationship between the reader and the author. Consult an attorney for specific information related to your personal legal situation.

Table of Contents

Part Two
BUILDING A FIREWALL: PROTECTING WHAT IS YOURS

Part Three
ALL HELL BREAKS LOOSE

About the Author

Coyt Randal Johnston believes that most of what you are told by his fellow lawyers, so-called investment gurus and number crunchers is meant to personally benefit those and the other professionals who rob you with a pen instead of a gun.

"It's funny how the prospect of a large financial gain will make people spin something as insidious as Enron into a benevolent enterprise bent on looking after the welfare of investors, their children and small pets," he says.

Randy Johnston is managing partner in the Dallas law firm of Johnston Tobey, P.C. For the past two decades, he has concentrated his practice on being a legal traffic cop who pulls over the worst offenders for professional malfeasance. Realizing that not every mistake is malpractice, Randy lectures to legal groups and does a monthly podcast for *Texas Lawyer* on legal ethics. His e-mail series, *Best Practices*, can be accessed from the law firm's Web site: www.johnstontobey.com

Randy has been selected for the list of Texas Super Lawyers featured in *Texas Monthly* since 2003 and is regularly chosen one of the Best Lawyers in Dallas by *D Magazine,* the city magazine of Dallas. He also was featured in 2007 in the *Go-To Guide* to Texas attorneys formulated by *American Lawyer*. Another local publication, *Dallas Observer*, featured him in 2008 as "the lawyer you would most like to hire to sue your lawyer."

Although *Robbed at Pen Point* is his first book of non-fiction, he is a published poet. He is also founder of Blue Collar Crime, a Texas Blues Brotherhood, a blues band that he calls "four lawyers and one guitar legend who needs four lawyers." You can learn more about his band by going to www.bluecollarcrime.com.

Randy is available to speak to groups on the subject of protecting yourself from scams and outrages at the hands of "The Suits." Contact him at 214 741-6260 or coytrandal@johnstontobey.com.

PROLOGUE

SOMETHING TO BELIEVE IN

We all want to have faith in something greater than ourselves. There's comfort in the knowledge that some force stronger, quicker and smarter than us will back our play.

For the young man in his cowboy suit on the opposite page (circa 1958), that force was the mythology of the Old West. Growing up in the oil and gas communities of West Texas, his inspiration was Audie Murphy, the little soldier who came to symbolize the fight against evil in a visceral and authentic way.

John Wayne made movies about heroism. Audie Murphy actually was a hero who jumped on a burning tank near a village in eastern France and saved his retreating buddies from German fire, and through his actions emerged the most decorated American soldier of World War II.

After the war, he reenacted that improbable scene in the movie, *To Hell and Back*, and played the hero in 40 other films, mostly westerns. The real story of Audie Murphy was less glamorous. For the remainder of his life, he was haunted by what we know was post-traumatic stress disorder so severe that he could only sleep with a loaded pistol under his pillow. Tragically, this bona fide hero died in a plane crash at age 46.

I knew all of this about Audie Murphy. My heart goes out to the troubled Audie, but the mythic one—the hired gun protecting those who couldn't protect themselves—was my hero. It was my desire to play the Audie Murphy part that brought me into the law a quarter century ago and compelled me to focus on protecting clients from those who rob at pen point. This book is an extension of that desire to protect. A frustrating limitation of the law is that I don't see these cases until the damage is already done. In order to warn about evildoers who want to take advantage of people, I blog and podcast to my fellow attorneys about this scourge and give speeches on the subject to industry groups and the general public, but that doesn't fix the problem.

With this book, I take it upon myself to let readers know how vulnerable you are to the machinations of unscrupulous professionals –lawyers, physicians, investment advisors, accountants, financial planners, fund managers, business partners and others who may owe you a fiduciary responsibility but will cheat you instead. They are The Suits who draw you into their evil orbit, only to take advantage of you in the end. With our latest financial calamity, you could add politicians to the list, for they are the enablers of all those other bad guys.

The victims of pen point thievery range from first-time investors to sophisticated veterans, from the very wealthy to those who wind up gambling away their kids' college savings and even their homes. I'll offer suggestions for avoiding trouble, the records you should keep and the questions you should ask. And I'll delve into your last resort: civil and criminal legal action. When is it necessary and how should you proceed?

Nothing is more satisfying than seeing that person you trusted and were stung by receive what he or she deserves, hopefully with some physical pain or financial despair thrown in. We will attempt to give you tools to make you successful against those who would harm you.

Thirteen Ways to Avoid
Being Robbed at Pen Point

The first part of this book deals with how we got to this point, having to worry about being robbed at pen point. The second part tells how to prevent the thievery. And the third part describes the many options available to you when you get burned and want to get even.

The following list presents some general rules for how to protect yourself from your own failings and the actions of scammers:

1. Regulate your greed. In most cases, a natural inclination to pursue unreasonable gains does us in.

2. If it sounds too good, it probably is. This should be the eleventh commandment, it's heard so often, but still we fall for it.

3. If you don't understand an investment, don't do it. Or if you don't understand what a doctor, lawyer or accountant wants to do on your behalf, forget about it.

4. Trust but verify.

5. No one will look after your welfare but you. With regulation a dirty word and ethics in the crapper, you can only get help after the fact, in the form of a lawsuit or grievance.

6. No professional is your friend. At least, that's not why that person is doing business with you. He or she is doing

it for money. That's not to say that you won't make friends with some professionals. But don't let friendship pressure you into doing something you otherwise would not do.

7. Consider all marketing claims to be lies until proven accurate. You should place the burden of proof on lawyers who make the many "Best of" lists.

8. Keep good records of all communications with professionals. Often this is helpful in establishing a pattern of negligent behavior.

9. Seek referrals when you are selecting a lawyer, doctor, investment counselor, accountant or other professional. Don't just hire the first person who cold calls you.

10. Don't be afraid to talk about the financial details with professionals of all kinds.

11. Don't buy investment products "on the margin." The system has the advantage and can wipe you out without your permission.

12. Be sure that you know the relationship between various professionals and how each of them is getting paid. You can bet the somehow you are paying all the freight.

13. Go into every deal with the understanding that if you get stiffed, you are not afraid to sue.

PART ONE

WHO DO YOU TRUST?

1

WHAT PASSES FOR
HONEST SERVICES?

Some years ago, author Joseph Heller was attending a cocktail party in the home of a billionaire Manhattan hedge fund manager when Heller's good friend, novelist Kurt Vonnegut, posed a question.

Vonnegut wanted to know what Heller thought about the fact that their host made more money in one day trading pieces of paper than Heller made on both the book and screenplay of his anti-war classic, *Catch 22*.

Heller knew this was certainly the case, but he told his friend that he had something the hedge fund manager couldn't possibly have.

"Enough," said Heller. He had enough. It was something he had in abundance and the hedge fund manager and many Americans would never have.

Each time I tell this story, I am reminded of Enron and its chief executive officer, Jeffrey Skilling. Here is a guy, like many top corporate executives, who could never have enough. As a result of trying to get more, he found himself before a three-judge panel of the 5th U.S. Circuit Court of Appeals. This court held Skilling's fate in their hands, and you couldn't help but notice: there wasn't the slightest hint of a wink or a nudge to his countenance. He was deadly serious that he was innocent. At issue was the appeal of Skilling's May 2006 conviction on 19 counts of fraud, conspiracy, insider trading and lying to auditors for his role in the collapse of Houston-based Enron, once the nation's seventh-largest company and now a charter member of the hall of shame for corporate recklessness on a massive scale.

Skilling's attorney admitted to the court that the former executive certainly took risks when he ran the company. In the theater of his mind, though, these risks were always for the benefit of the company and not for any tawdry self-aggrandizement.

The Enron story brings to mind some of the more oxymoronic constructs of our no-amount-of-money-is-ever-enough culture. There's the medical one about how the operation was successful but the patient died. Or the Vietnam era inanity: We had to destroy the village to save it. Somewhere in all of this, common sense has got to reassert itself.

Prosecutors in Skilling's trial argued, among other theories, that the defendant deprived Enron of his honest services. The fact that his company went belly-up while he got rich proves that he didn't exactly sacrifice himself to save the little guy's bacon.

What everyone seems to forget these days is that a corporation *is* the shareholders, not the officers and directors. They include all of us, from fat-cat dot-com zillionaires to teachers' pension programs to employees who trust their careers and retirement to the intentions of executives like Skilling and his mates. Corporate toadies love to remind us of this when they want to cut corporate tax rates, but they somehow forget it when it is time to divvy up massive corporate profits.

Skilling's scene took place in the spring of 2008. Whether he lives out his original 24-year sentence at a federal correctional facility in Minnesota or goes home tomorrow, ask yourself this question: How high up the ladder do you need to be, how much information must you have and what power over company developments should you exercise to be held accountable? Is anyone ever at fault?

In the great gazillion-dollar financial crisis of 2008, which at this writing is still developing, fault takes a back seat to the immediate danger of the situation. Everyone is angry at greedy Wall Street bankers, regulators asleep at the switch and predatory politicians. But when people say there is plenty of blame to go around, you can bet the blame never gets around and no one but the victims pay.

We thought Enron, Tyco, WorldCom and others represented corporate malfeasance on the grandest scale, leading to the loss of thousands of jobs, stock being devalued into the billions and the disappearance of employee pension plans.

But you could say Skilling and his brother felons stole too *little* to get the attention they deserve compared to the hundreds of billions of dollars tied up in the current mortgage/credit/financial mess. The genius of this latest crop of thieves is that they were deemed too big and important to fail. In their avarice, they tied their fate to the welfare of millions of homeowners, investors and taxpayers.

Be Your Own Best Financial Advisor

Why are these stories of high corporate and governmental crime so important? What does it teach us about the world at large? The lesson is deceptively simple: you must look out for your own best financial interests because no one else will. Companies may look solid. Deals may appear fair until you really examine the fundamentals.

Those people who are supposedly looking out for you? They are busy tending to their own interests, and sooner or later their interests will collide with yours. Which do you think will take precedence?

Once I saw a report on one of those television magazine shows about a boiler room operation that specialized in stealing money from the poor and elderly. The telephone solicitor/thief was getting all emotional about the fact that he could get these old ladies to do anything for him. Draw money out of their accounts and send it to him. Talk their friends into signing over their property.

The man was tearfully retelling the tale, but the tears weren't for his victims. He sobbed that he needed the money for his wife's cancer treatment. He had no other choice but to do the morally repugnant thing. But he was willing to do it for *his* family, as if invoking family made his acts more humane. The only way he knew how to cure his difficulty was to harm others. To his way of thinking, his financial interests trumped those of the vulnerable people he bilked over the phone.

Fortunately, every deal does not rip off every consumer. But some businesspeople can't seem to help themselves. They press beyond the ethical limits and take advantage of the individual, in hopes of windfall profits. Guys like this play the *rules*, not the *game*.

In most cases, it is the most mundane action on your part that triggers your victimization: signing your name. With a pen stroke, you give your word to abide by a specific agreement. The other party to the agreement, be it a national corporation, an accountant down the block or even a lawyer who promises to help, does the same. But was the deal fair or even legal? Did you have all the information necessary to make an informed decision or did the other side in this transaction successfully keep vital facts from you? Did the professional hold up his end of the bargain or tip the playing field in an unlevel manner? Too often, the consumer learns the answer too late.

When a transaction takes a wayward turn, the victim may end up thinking he or she was stupid to trust the other guy. Prospective clients sit in my conference room and tell me horrible stories of pen point theft, and often they end by blaming themselves. Usually the victim can take a small percentage of the fault, but not all of it. Average working people must operate in a world where the push for short-term, bottom-line results by well organized bad guys can overwhelm all else. The consumer usually takes the punch. Sometimes it's swift, too fast to dodge. Other times, it's a haymaker. You see the windup. You feel the wind against your face, but you can't get out of the way.

Ever try to clear up a billing error with AT&T or Citibank or one of any number of those robotic corporate entities? To do so you enter an entirely new era of what passes for customer service. First off, if your dispute does not fit within the seven or eight voicemail prompts that comprise their automated response system, you are out of luck. Everyone knows that most customer service departments are outsourced to India or Pakistan. Workers on the sales side of those operations are highly trained to respond to the American vernacular. The latest gambit, though, is to staff the complaint departments with people who speak little or no English. Talk about your gripes falling on deaf ears! And even if you get an English speaker, once that person realizes you are not purchasing anything additional, the great grey curtain of corporate indifference closes around you.

We are the big corporation. If you terminate service, we charge you. If you continue service, we charge you. You want to sue us? We will make you arbitrate in our hometown. Oh, you won't buy our services again? Ok, you are just one of millions. Besides, we can sell ourselves to another company or change our name and then you will buy from us again.

Learning Their Thieving Ways From Corporations

This book is not aimed so much at helping you deal with large corporations as it is helping you with the individual attorney, stockbroker or business manager. The point is that many individuals hiding behind contracts pattern themselves after the way corporations have gone from serving us to mastering us over the past couple of decades. There is a profound paradigm shift at work in people's dealings with others. In search of profits, both corporations and individuals have become more impersonal and less responsive and that can only lead to more problems with customer service up and down the line. While most free-market societies have moved toward more protections for the consumer, in the U.S. we have moved backward toward the doctrine of caveat emptor, let the buyer beware.

Here's the hard reality: In this world, we're each the little guy. No matter how many BMWs sit in your driveway or how many zeroes there are in your checking account balance, The Suits and the institutions they control can get to you.

2

THE CASE FOR CAUTION

Oregon rancher Loyd Stubbs was a nineteenth century man adrift in a sea of modern situational ethics. A sheepherder for most of his life, Stubbs didn't seem like the type of person a con man would take the time to cheat. The old man lived on a monthly pension check of $640 until his brother and ranching partner died in 1998. The two brothers owned a ranch near the small town of Brownsville, Oregon and suddenly Loyd Stubbs found himself with close to a half-million dollars in cash and other assets that his brother had accumulated.

The money only confused him, like most things these days. As he passed his 87th birthday, the old man wasn't thinking too clearly. So when local financial advisor and estate planner John Williams suggested he take that money for Stubbs and invest it, the old rancher was relieved.

Every so often, Williams would drive 30 miles north on the Pacific Highway out of Eugene to the ranch off the interstate between Halsey and Sweet Home. He would place a sheaf of papers before the elderly, confused man, who didn't know much about contracts, agreements and waivers. Stubbs wouldn't know what it was if he read it, so he just signed the papers.

Some time later, a family member told a Eugene newspaper reporter that Stubbs "was old-fashioned. Everything was done with a handshake. If he trusted you, he trusted you explicitly." The younger investment advisor was like a son to the old man, or so he thought. Only later was the extent of Williams' treachery revealed.

Members of the Stubbs family began to wonder about the money as their elderly relative's health declined and they felt the need to spend time with him. He couldn't really tell them where the money was, but at first they just figured he misplaced his bank passbook and it would turn up. The last person who would warrant suspicion was John Williams. Here was a man of impeccable reputation in the area, actively involved in church and community affairs. No one had ever questioned his credibility as an investment counselor or as a human being.

But John Anthony Williams, as he would later be referred to in news stories, had a dream that lived in the darkest part of his heart. While the details of his dream were uniquely his, the core of the dream is actually quite common: he would do anything to become rich. This particular dream included living in a new country, with a new wife and a new identity. The dream required lots of money; as it turned out, he would need other peoples' money. Soon after Loyd Stubbs received his inheritance, Williams sold the elderly man an annuity and earned himself a $30,000 commission. But that was chump change to a man with a dream.

According to Assistant United States Attorney Chris Cardani, Williams' dealings showed him how vulnerable the old man was and Williams determined that Stubbs' money was enough to fund whatever his imagination could create. In July 1999, Williams obtained a power of attorney, naming himself as the octogenarian's agent for all financial affairs. Williams then used that power of attorney to open a private mailbox in Stubbs' name, as well as a bank account in both of their names. Williams then had Loyd Stubbs sign a number of documents, some of which cancelled the same annuities he had sold the elderly gentleman. Williams faxed these documents and the power of attorney to the annuity company, requesting that the face value of the policies, $415,000, be sent immediately to the new joint bank account. All the while, Stubbs didn't have a clue that he was being robbed at pen point. That's one of the common aspects to this type of crime: if someone sticks a gun in your ribs, you know immediately that you are in trouble. When they use a pen, you may not know it for years.

As instructed, the annuity company liquidated the policies and transferred the proceeds. Here's where Williams' dream scenario plays into the action. He quickly moved the funds to his own bank account. Then he formed an offshore company in the Central American country of Belize, opened a bank account at the Bank of Belize and wire transferred the tainted funds to the bank. In October 1999, Williams went to Belize, purchased a beachfront condominium, and lived there for six months.

Williams knew that banking secrecy laws in Belize would help him if he was caught, but apparently he decided that wiping the slate clean was a better move. Everything had gone so smoothly to this point that he apparently got a little cocky. He took a chance on returning to Oregon in July 2000, intent on causing the name and identity of John Anthony Williams to vanish into thin air. It almost worked, but local police detained him when he attempted to obtain a social security card in a false name.

Williams had several pieces of false identification from Belize when he was arrested. Eventually, he admitted that he intended to move out of the United States using the identity he so creatively concocted. Williams pleaded guilty to (get this!) misdemeanor identity theft in state court.

Even then, no one was aware that Williams had stolen $415,000 from Loyd Stubbs. In 2002—almost three years after Williams absconded with the inheritance—a suspicious relative notified the Federal Bureau of Investigation. The FBI then began to unravel the web of financial transactions initiated by Williams to commit the fraud and keep it a secret.

In April 2004, after a three-day trial, a jury in federal court convicted Williams on four counts of wire fraud, three counts of mail fraud, three counts of money laundering and one count of foreign transportation of stolen money. He was sentenced to four years and three months in prison and ordered to pay full restitution.

Thanks to the efforts of the skilled attorneys representing Loyd Stubbs, most of his lost money has been reimbursed by the annuity company. Some of it also came from the malpractice insurance company for the lawyer who drafted most of the paperwork that Williams got Loyd Stubbs to sign.

Yes, an attorney was involved in the theft, and he hasn't escaped this fiasco. In most cases, a con man will falsify his own documents unless he can hook up with an attorney who will enable his actions. James Britt was a Eugene attorney who shared office space with Williams when he unknowingly assisted in the robbery of Loyd Stubbs.

Information from the Oregon State Bar shows that Williams originally asked Britt to represent Stubbs by preparing amendments to the elderly man's trust that added the planner as a trustee. Britt also prepared the power of attorney appointing the planner as attorney in fact.

Britt had limited experience at what he was doing and he committed an unpardonable sin for a lawyer. He let Williams direct his representation on behalf of Stubbs, who was the client. Determining exactly who an attorney represents is often an important factor in cases of legal malpractice. Amazingly enough, Britt never met or spoke with his client or verified his client's mental capacity. He did not know first-hand if his client even existed.

At Williams' request, lawyer Britt also prepared a letter verifying that Stubbs wanted to give the financial planner a large amount of money as a gift. The letter maintained that the elderly man was fully capable of understanding what he was doing. Britt knew Williams intended to have Stubbs sign the letter. The planner would present it to third parties who would rely on the attorney's representations, and this would probably lead to other business dealings favorable to Williams.

Britt admitted he had become suspicious of Williams and that he even knew some of his own representations were false. He also knew that he didn't have enough information to say what he said in the documents, but he never took the time to get the correct information and none of this stopped him, or even slowed him down, from doing the work to help Williams rob at pen point.

In 2006, the Oregon Bar's disciplinary board found Britt guilty of dishonesty or misrepresentation, failure to provide competent representation and avoiding influence by others than the client. His law license was suspended for six months.

The board determined that Britt did not intend to cause his client harm and did not knowingly conspire with Williams to steal the elderly man's funds. Britt simply allowed himself to be manipulated to the detriment of his client, and only his inexperience and the fact that he cooperated with authorities to reveal this tragedy kept his punishment from being more severe.

Numerous attorneys for the companies involved aided Stubbs in getting his money back, but the one in a position to protect him from Williams failed him miserably. Of course, the old man never had the satisfaction of seeing James Britt get his punishment. Loyd Stubbs died in 2005 at the age of 93.

We Worship the Gods And Goddess of Success

The point of the Loyd Stubbs' story is something you know in your bones – that rogues exist, from individuals to conglomerates, and societal changes have allowed them to flourish. They may be world-beating corporations or trusted advisors who run off with the money. They may be the well-heeled seeking every advantage to add more wealth, even attorneys who fail to uphold their responsibilities.

You have to ask yourself why already-successful individuals would take a chance on bending laws and ignoring moral standards in hope of nudging their personal wealth up just a notch or two? After all, most of us lead more comfortable lives than ever before. The average home in this country is larger than ever before, and even the cheapest automobiles come with a diverse assortment of gadgetry not even imagined by our grandparents. Americans in the lower socio-economic groups carry cell phones and iPods and wear high-dollar running shoes. Rich or poor, we all seem to be engaged in a dizzying race to own more stuff. A friend of mine once noted, "We spend money we don't have to buy things we don't need to impress people we don't know."

Even the most meager household income in this country is off the chart compared with most of the world. More than two-thirds of the nation's residents have become homeowners. And the upper one-third of wage earners, according to the U.S. Census Bureau, earned an average of $57,660 in 2005. Those numbers are impressive, but they don't mean much when they bump up against expectations. Even with all of our largesse, there are pressures on wage earners, who have actually seen slight erosion in buying power over the past 40 years.

A major concern of economists is the growing income gap. The median household income for the top 20% of wage earners in 2000 was 14 times higher than that of the bottom 20%. By 2004, the top group earned 14.8 times more than the lower. By 2005, the top 20% of households claimed more than half of all income.

The growing disparity in incomes gives rise to the robbed at pen point mindset. Expectations lead to a sense of entitlement. One person fights tooth and nail to gain greater economic status. Someone else struggles just to hold ground. And everyone must work, shop and live within this overheated environment, where shortcuts too often seem the only method for climbing one rung higher on the economic ladder.

The intensity of concern for our own financial condition is heightened because every function of man or government is reduced to a price tag. We are told how much it costs to raise a child or to retire. The price of gasoline is with us as much as our cholesterol numbers. George W. Bush, who should have been overseeing the financial health of all Americans, described those closest to him as "the haves and the have-mores." With only obscene wealth understood as worthwhile, it's easy to see how people unable to obtain such wealth without cheating would feel completely justified.

There's That Dirty Word, "Regulation"

A fine line exists between healthy business success and obscene wealth, the wealth that equals celebrity. As a nation and a society, we function best when those pushing the edge of the envelope possess an appreciation for right and wrong. Business has always pushed the boundaries and should do so. That's not necessarily bad. An aggressive business community vitalizes the economy with benefits for all. But within this system, there must be forces that provide checks and balances to create equilibrium between fairness and windfall. That is where we have fallen down: only since the latest financial crisis has "regulation" transformed itself from a curse word into a mantra of what's reasonable.

Government regulatory agencies and the courts have historically provided that needed backstop, reminding business not to go too far, but the balance shifted after 1980. That's the year Ronald Reagan and his band of economic conservatives took power after many decades in the wilderness. "Morning in America," for the most part, was a call to the natural creativity and solid work ethic in the American people. But it also had its dark side, as most movements do. It meant that those in charge of market oversight were so blinded by the bright sunrise that they couldn't notice thieves in the kitchen.

President Reagan lifted the spirits of a nation that was souring on itself, and I respect him for that, but Reaganites gleefully set out to shut down government from the moment they came into office. From their first days, though, they found the bureaucracy so entrenched that it was impossible to actually kill the beast they all hated. Powerful members of Congress had their favorite programs and were willing to fight for them. This job was more difficult than they ever imagined and would take decades to accomplish.

The first step was to severely weaken many of the federal agencies so they could not do what they were mandated to do. From the National Labor Relations Board to the Securities and Exchange Commission, "job one" was to make these agencies do their jobs badly. This was done primarily by cutting budgets to the point that they could not function properly. The second step, after showing how awful government can be, was to complain about its lack of effectiveness.

The prophesy was indeed self-fulfilling. If you purposely run an agency into the ground by shutting off its funds, it will inspire a lot of complaints. Their genius was the ability to conflate the two ideas without the public realizing they were the very ones responsible for the inability of government to respond to the citizens' needs. Economic Katrina!

By the time George W. Bush came to power in 2001, elimination of all regulatory authority was the goal. Bush's own economic mini-me, tax hater Grover Norquist, put it best. He proposed to shrink government "down to the size where we can drown it in the bathtub…" Think about that in light of this country's venerable tradition of "government of the people, by the people and for the people." A result was the actual Katrina!

With such an obsession, the Bushies (Karl Rove's word, not mine) were perfectly happy to let the fox visit the henhouse unaccompanied. When the home mortgage crisis began to take shape, conservatives wanted to blame it all on obscure legislation from more than three decades ago that encouraged poor people to purchase homes. But this wasn't the fault of any one law from the right or left. You can lay the blame on a philosophy that entails identifying those you consider the smartest guys in the room, providing them with maximum funding and getting out of their way. It is based on voluntary regulation, an oxymoron if I've ever heard one.

I recall an unrelated policy choice back when George W. Bush was governor of Texas that showcases his attitude toward regulation. At one point, Gov. Bush responded to the tightly restricted use of state funds by school districts by proposing grants that would allow individual districts to decide how this grant money would be used in pursuit of better education. It all sounded good, allowing local control and giving school administrators freedom of choice in deciding how to disburse money to improve the education of our kids.

"These are good people, hard-working folks. Trust them to use that money wisely. We don't want any bureaucrat from Austin gummin' up the works, tellin' 'em how to spend their money."

Only problem was, with no one looking over their shoulder, many school boards across the state used that money to hire a 12th or 13th

football coach or provide bonuses for a few favored administrators. Very little of that money went toward programs emphasizing educational excellence, and people across the state who funded the grants wondered what this incompetence had to do with the Republican ideal of fiscal discipline.

On the national level, the Bushies added a layer of hypocrisy that the Reaganites never envisioned and principled conservatives find incredible today. While decrying regulation, undermining the ability of government to solve problems (again, Katrina) and giving lip service to the mantra of eliminating "waste, fraud and abuse," they have overseen the most massive expansion of government power in our history. And, you may ask, for what purpose?

As the credit crunch and mortgage crisis was unfolding, the Bush Administration showed that it never learned its lesson. An editorial in *The New York Times* titled "Not Much of a Watchdog" pointed out

"...even as the financial sector's recklessness is tipping the economy into crisis, the Securities and Exchange Commission seems to be bending over backward to not discomfit the banks and firms it regulates....Like other regulatory agencies, the SEC's enforcement division has had its budget cut in recent years and its staffing level has dropped, making it harder to do the necessary work. But staff lawyers also complain of commissioners overruling the findings of the SEC's enforcement division to water down fines and payments. In one instance, JP Morgan Chase had agreed to pay a $25 million settlement only to have the commissioners overrule the deal, reducing the bill to $2 million." It reminds me of the cartoon where a Coast Guard helicopter arrives at a sinking ship, with lots of people in the water, and announces, "we are here to save the manufacturer and the captain of the ship."

Most Americans learned from this crisis that the idea of regulating business interests resided far down the list of Bush's favorite government responsibilities, just below "place head in sand in response to calamity." But even he had to take notice after the housing crisis and credit crunch began to wreak havoc on the economy and the lives of our fellow countrymen.

Ninety-nine percent of the time, relaxing regulations leads to positive results. That's a fact. But reasonable regulation is aimed at curbing the outlaw one percent when the powers that be invariably go too far and steal so blatantly that even the most die-hard free market capitalist is offended. Lack of oversight can begin a cycle of corruption. As soon as one person steals and gets away with it, everyone else feels free to do the same. After all, if a business ignores a possible advantage, can it continue to operate? Consider what would happen if one business were allowed to dump untreated waste into the neighboring river: that company would prosper while the companies who paid to treat their waste would decline. At the company's annual meeting, the shareholders of the responsible firm would want to know why the company hired a CEO who was ruining the company and their investment. Reasonable regulation by the government is necessary to level the playing field and keep businesses from devolving toward the lowest common denominator of ethics.

Back to our thesis that enough is often not enough: in 2006, Michael O. Pickens, the son of billionaire energy magnate T. Boone Pickens, admitted to participating in a scheme to inflate the stock value of three companies. Prosecutors argued he sent hundreds of thousands of faxes drafted to look like handwritten notes, passing along stock tips that were "accidentally" going to the wrong recipient. People who received these faxes thought they had been let in on a great stock tip, the chance of a lifetime. The idea was to build excitement for the stock with people who thought they had stumbled onto a golden stock tip, pump up the price and then sell the stock for a profit. It is called a "pump and dump." You probably received a "pump and dump" email today.

Pickens the younger understood the powerful lure of a stock tip, especially from someone with his last name. It's a play meant to tickle the basic greed in all of us; most of us like to believe we are immune from such enticements. In reality, though, greed represents a deep well in all of us, too easily tapped into by those able to take advantage.

And that completes the circle of financial life: economic factors create this predatory monster that is not being policed by the government and it latches on to the naïve and greedy. But wait, there is more. When government fails to do its job, the court system still stands strong as protector of the victims, right? Well, not so much anymore.

The Attack on Our Courts

Frustrated.

That's apparently how Senator John Cornyn felt on a spring day in 2005 when he came to the U.S. Senate chamber to blame judges for the very violence aimed at those same judges, due to their "raw or ideological decisions." That's right, following a shooting at a state courthouse, this Republican member of the Senate Judiciary Committee blamed the judges that were targeted for murder. He sharply criticized a ruling of the U.S. Supreme Court on the death penalty. And he blamed "activist judges" for recent violence against jurists and their families.

Said Cornyn:

> "It causes a lot of people, including me, great distress to see judges use the authority that they have been given to make raw political or ideological decisions….the Supreme Court has taken

on this role as a policymaker rather than an enforcer of political decisions made by elected representatives of the people.

"I don't know if there is a cause-and-effect connection, but we have seen some recent episodes of courthouse violence in this country.... And I wonder whether there may be some connection between the perception in some quarters, on some occasions, where judges are making political decisions yet are unaccountable to the public, that it builds up and builds up and builds up to the point where some people engage in violence. Certainly without any justification, but a concern that I have."

It was a stunning accusation by a political figure such as Cornyn, who formerly served on his state supreme court. It followed on the heels of two fatal episodes that made headlines that year. In Chicago, a man fatally shot the husband and mother of a federal judge who had ruled against him in a medical malpractice case. In Atlanta the month before, a man broke away from police and killed four people, including the judge who presided over his rape trial.

Cornyn seemed to be siding with homicidal maniacs in these cases, excusing their violence, blaming it on the judges themselves. Here he was justifying violence against judges based on decisions by the highest court in the land, which was overwhelmingly appointed by presidents of his own political party (seven appointed by Republicans, two by Democrats). Oh yes, and the decision he was so unhappy with: a ruling that it was unconstitutional for the state of Texas to execute minors.

His remarks followed those by House Majority Leader Tom DeLay, who also condemned judges involved in the case of the brain-damaged Florida woman, Terry Schiavo. The Republican Party had made this poor woman's situation a cause celebre. Yet every judge who heard the actual facts of the case ruled against the parents and in favor of her husband, who wanted to allow her to die. Every judge – state, federal, Democrat, Republican, trial level or appeal – did their duty to enforce the constitution and interpret the law fairly and came to the same conclusion.

"The time will come for the men responsible for this to answer for their behavior," DeLay said. The warning was clear: he wanted substantive changes in the oversight of judges. Delay and his supporters were asking for the right to sue judges over their rulings. They sought a clear and easy path to recall judges, removing them from the bench. And judicial term limits. Anything to make judges respond to political pressure.

Criticism of Cornyn for his remarks was fairly resounding, and the American Bar Association (ABA) set out to squelch talk of any change to the judicial appointment system. The ABA produced a film called "Countering the Critics," for screenings nationally at churches, civic clubs and chambers of commerce. They created media kits and pamphlets intended to educate the public and thereby address the attacks. The ABA came to the defense of judges when the other branches of government turned on them.

An excerpt from one sample opinion editorial from the ABA's Kit on Fair and Impartial Courts illustrates the ABA's arguments:

> "Recent criticism of judges has crossed the line from healthy debate to judge bashing that threatens the fairness and impartiality of our courts. Politicians and interest groups regularly issue dark warnings to judges, simply because they disagree with the judges' decisions.
>
> "There is no place for this in our country. A fair and impartial judiciary is essential to democracy and protects our rights under the Constitution. Attempts to intimidate judges are efforts to

influence their decisions. If we let external pressure tip the scales of justice, we will lose the one place where we all can be heard on an equal footing.

"When our Founders wrote the Constitution, they purposely shielded courts from political influence so judges could protect our freedom – a revolutionary idea. Before then, courts too often were manipulated by the rich and powerful seeking to protect their interests and deny justice to those they had wronged. We created a system where judges are different; they consider only the facts and the law in making their decisions, which gives all of us our day in court. We must not turn back the clock to the days of justice only for the few and privileged because of a handful of decisions the few and privileged dislike."

For awhile, the country actually seemed on the verge of agreement with Delay and Cornyn. We actually had to ask ourselves if weakening the court system could create a better world for the individual. In the end, though, the public decided that we like our judges and the system of courts. The backlash from the Schiavo case and the loss of Congress by the Republicans in 2006 made this issue go away. We decided that if one of the rogues – emboldened by the lack of judicial review – knocked on our door, we wanted the court system to protect us.

The average consumer has a love-hate relationship with the nation's system of torts, which encompasses all negligence cases as well as claims involving intentional wrongs that cause harm. Claims might include those against hospitals for negligence, against a stockbroker for churning a client's account or against a lawyer for stealing the proceeds of a client's insurance settlement. On the one hand, the tort system can be a bulwark against the steamroller of big businesspeople in suits. Torts provide a way to recoup direct losses, such as repayments of missed wages and monetary penalties to deter a business from continuing to harm individuals. The tort system, though, has come under a fire as hot as that affecting judges, with certain cases reaching iconic status as frivolous lawsuits. Thanks to late-night television hosts, litigation involving McDonald's hot coffee (see sidebar) or junk food that makes people fat has inspired changes in our laws and caps in monetary awards.

Texas voters approved tort reform legislation in 2003. The action limited non-economic damages such as pain and suffering in medical malpractice cases to $250,000 per case or $750,000 when there are multiple defendants.

Other states also cap non-economic damages, with each state determining the specifics: Alaska, California, Colorado, Florida, Georgia, Hawaii, Idaho, Illinois, Kansas, Maryland, Massachusetts, Michigan, Mississippi, Missouri, Montana, Nevada, North Dakota, Ohio, Oklahoma, Oregon, South Carolina, South Dakota, Utah, West Virginia and Wisconsin.

Five states also place a cap on total damages: Colorado, Indiana, Louisiana, Nebraska, New Mexico and Virginia.

Think about what these caps really do; they take away the power of the jury to determine your loss! Remember Senator Cornyn and his gripe with the Supreme Court? Senator Cornyn criticized the U.S. Supreme Court's 5 to 4 decision holding that it was unconstitutional to *execute people under age 18* with the following observation:

> "In so holding, the U.S. Supreme Court said 'we are no longer going to leave this in the hands of jurors.'"

Cornyn has been a big supporter of caps on malpractice claims and other restrictions on the ability of people to sue for damages. Isn't it ironic that the Good Senator trusts jurors to take away a boy's life if he kills someone, but he does not trust the same jury to take away a doctor's money if the doctor kills someone!!!

Texas now has one of the most restrictive cap systems in America, which lawmakers sold to voters by emphasizing that awards exceeding caps just show greed. This may sound reasonable. Why should an individual get millions of dollars for their pain and suffering? Lost wages, sure, that we understand, but not pain and suffering.

The discrimination inherent in the caps system borders on state-sponsored brutality. For example, say you are a 38-year-old corporate executive who earns $350,000 a year. You go to the hospital for routine surgery but a sponge is accidentally left in the wound, causing infection, extended hospitalization, a second surgery and some disability. Under Texas law, you can sue the hospital for $250,000 for pain and suffering *and* a separate amount for all your lost income. You are a moneymaking dynamo compared with other Americans. You have been climbing the corporate ladder since you graduated from college and you have plenty of assets for your effort. No cap restricts your lost income recovery. If you are unable to work, the doctor, the hospital and everyone involved with this mishap will pay well into the millions for your economic damages.

What's perverse about this situation is that the burden of the cap is borne by those least able to afford it. That includes the elderly, the physically and mentally handicapped and the poor. Say you are a stay-at-home mom who cares for three small children as well as your elderly mother. You are burned in a household fire, but the situation is made worse by the inadequate treatment you receive from an emergency physician. After all your scars and time in a hospital's burn unit, you can only sue for $250,000, because you have no lost income. The benefits you contribute to society are incalculable and the amount your family must pay to substitute for your work is immense. But you have no income, and under state law that's all that matters. From a $250,000 award, you must subtract the cost of expert witnesses as well as the attorneys' fees and the fact that state law requires the plaintiff to prove significant parts of the case just to be allowed in court. If you should win, your attorney will take between 30% and half the amount of the verdict. Many defendants with the deepest pockets will appeal as a way to avoid payment. And once on appeal, the state supreme court has reversed many verdicts as excessive. It's a long, hard slog with only a small chance of recovery.

Voting Away Our Rights

The passage of Proposition 12 to the Texas Constitution capping non-economic damages in medical malpractice cases proves a valuable political lesson; no alien force can curtail our liberties more effectively than we can ourselves with the simple act of voting. A razor-thin majority of voters bought the argument that Prop 12 would bring greater access to health care and reduce costs. Four years later, many doctors with malpractice claims against them in other jurisdictions have moved to Texas in droves. They are protected by this law from the consequences of their ignorance and incompetence; and doctors' insurance rates have not even come down proportionally.

Texas Trial Lawyers Association President Paul Waldner says the law has accomplished only one goal, reducing the frequency of claims on behalf of injured patients.

> "As was anticipated," says Waldner, "serious injuries inflicted on children, stay-at-home moms, the elderly – those patients who are outside the work force and suffer no economic loss – it's more and more difficult for them to get legal representation, irrespective of how gross the malpractice may be."

In jurisdictions all across the nation, the burden of covering loss by our most vulnerable citizens has shifted away from corporations responsible for those losses. Lawyers are reluctant to accept cases that may not cover medical bills and expert witness fees, much less their own expenses. So the result is clear, and those who support tort reform have cleverly masked what they are doing. By convincing the public that plaintiffs' trial lawyers are the scum of the earth, they have closed off a judicial safety net to those who need it the most.

Think again about the limits of what a jury can do for the most seriously injured of our fellow citizens. Imagine two people hurt by medical malpractice; one spends a few days in the hospital, gets well, goes home and resumes his or her life. The other is hurt horribly, spends months in the hospital, lives a life of constant pain and dies a year later of these injuries. The jury can make whole the one who is barely hurt by awarding damages under the cap. But the one who will die young and live in constant pain until that death is the person whose money is capped.

It's not a matter of who is hurt, but who is hurt most expensively. If our doctors screw up a little, we are prepared to take care of that. But if they mess up big time, the state protects the doctors from that responsibility. That, brothers and sisters, is cruel, no matter what your political persuasion. It is hypocrisy at the highest levels.

The Real Story
Of A Famous 'Frivolous' Lawsuit

To test your legal knowledge, select the most correct option below. As we know them, frivolous lawsuits are

a.) Greatly misunderstood
b.) Lawsuits brought by people other than yourself
c.) Great fun for late night comedians
d.) The reason tort reform laws are being passed
e.) All of the above.

If you answered "e", you are correct. And the king of the lawsuits deemed frivolous, the one that still gets attention many years after the incident happened, is simply known as McDonald's Hot Coffee.

What do you know about the McDonald's case? Millions of Americans who think they know this story recount that a woman spilled some McDonald's coffee on herself, got burned and a jury gave her beaucoup bucks.

Poor McDonald's, poor business in general. Let's pass laws to prevent that injustice from ever happening again.

The way the real story goes, 79-year-old Stella Liebeck of Albuquerque, New Mexico was in the passenger seat when her grandson drove his car into the drive-thru lane of a McDonald's restaurant in February 1992.

Liebeck ordered coffee, which was served in a styrofoam cup. After she received the order, the grandson moved his car forward and stopped for her to add sugar and cream to her coffee. Rumor had it that Liebeck was driving and the car was moving, but that was wrong.

While not driving and not moving, the elderly woman was unable to find a level surface on which to place the cup, which was getting hotter to the touch. So she placed the cup between her knees and tried to remove the plastic lid. As she did that, the contents of the cup spilled into her lap. The coffee was estimated at between 180 and 190 degrees.

Later, a vascular surgeon diagnosed Liebeck as having third-degree burns over her inner thighs, perineum, buttocks, and genital and groin areas. The burns extended through to her subcutaneous fat, muscle and bone. She was hospitalized for eight days and underwent skin grafting and other treatments. She was permanently disfigured in those areas and disabled for two years as a result of the injury.

A retired department store clerk, Liebeck informed McDonald's of her accident and requested that the fast food giant *simply* pay her medical bills totaling $11,000. She didn't demand payment for pain and suffering. She didn't feign economic damages. She simply wanted them to reimburse her out-of-pocket medical expenses. It all could have stopped here, but McDonald's refused.

With the restaurant company stonewalling her, Liebeck decided to contact a lawyer to help her collect those medical expenses. This lawyer had represented a woman several years earlier in a similar case against McDonald's, in which a quality assurance manager for the company testified that "he was aware of this risk ... and had no plans to turn down the heat."

The lawyer settled that case with McDonald's for $27,500. Before filing suit, the lawyer asked McDonald's to pay $90,000 for Liebeck's medical expenses and pain and suffering. The fast food giant could, once again, have compromised for a much smaller amount, but they chose instead to insult the woman by offering $800.

Liebeck had never been involved in a legal matter before, but McDonald's dismissive manner caused her to file suit in 1993, alleging the coffee she purchased was defective because of excessive heat and inadequate warnings. She also sought punitive damages based on her belief that McDonald's acted with conscious indifference to the safety of its customers.

Just before trial, the lawyer offered to settle for $300,000 and reportedly would have settled for half that amount. A mediator recommended a $225,000 settlement but McDonald's—although seeing their exposure rise before their very eyes—refused to budge.

During seven days of trial, the evidence against McDonald's was awfully damning, including:

- Between 1982 and 1992, more than 700 claims for similar injuries caused by their hot coffee were brought against McDonald's, claims settled for a total of more than $500,000.
- It was McDonald's policy to serve all coffee at approximately 185 degrees, even though they knew coffee at this temperature would cause scalding injuries to the mouth and throat of the consumer.
- McDonald's prepared its coffee at almost boiling temperature (212 degrees Fahrenheit) and served it between 180 and 190 degrees because research told them their customers want it "steamy hot," a merchandising decision that trumped safety.
- The company considered the 700 burn claims "statistically insignificant" when compared to the one billion cups of coffee sold each year by McDonald's.
- McDonald's chose not to warn their customers about the coffee because they felt there were more serious dangers in restaurants.

In rebuttal, McDonald's attorneys argued that Liebeck contributed to her injuries by placing the cup between her legs and by not "removing her clothing" promptly after the spill. Now that would be a unique warning: *Must remove clothing to safely drink coffee.*

Once the jury got the case, they found that McDonald's was liable on the claims of product defect, breach of the implied warranty of merchantability, and breach of the implied warranty of fitness for a particular purpose.

They awarded Liebeck $200,000 in compensatory damages, but reduced that amount to $160,000 because they felt the elderly woman was 20% at fault for the injuries. Then they awarded Liebeck $2.7 million in punitive damages, about two days of revenue from coffee sales for McDonald's.

That brought the total award to just under $3 million but Liebeck didn't just walk away from the courtroom with that much money. First, the trial judge reduced the total award to $640,000. Then he ordered the parties to engage in a post-verdict settlement conference, knowing that Liebeck was serious about wanting redress and McDonald's would probably appeal the verdict until the elderly woman was either deceased or physically unable to proceed.

After two-and-one-half years of living with injury and what she considered injustice, Liebeck settled with McDonald's for something less than $600,000. As a result, McDonald's didn't change its policy on the temperature of its coffee, but many McDonald's drive-thrus posted signs warning that their coffee is VERY HOT. Also, the plastic lids for hot beverage cups are marked HOT! HOT! HOT! They still hand this super-heated coffee out the window to you in your car, with the cream and sugar you requested on top, so that you have no choice but to take off the lid in your car to insert your cream and sugar, while they encourage you to hurry up and move along so they can serve the customer in the car behind you. They could, of course, have their employees serve you coffee the way you ordered it, with cream and sugar inside the cup, but that would take too long. So, instead, they make you do it in your car, with a liquid that is so hot that it is unfit for human consumption.

More was accomplished here than just giving David Letterman fodder for his late night monologue. It didn't bring big business to its knees, crippling them as most tort reformers claim. It didn't extort money on behalf of some predatory lay-about with no socially redeeming value. But it did cause a major corporation that affects the lives of many Americans to consider what can happen when they disregard the safety of those customers.

3

WHEN KNOWING RIGHT
FROM WRONG ISN'T
SO SIMPLE

To Alvin Berry, life boils down to a few fundamental lessons we all learned as children. Take responsibility for your actions. Accomplishments earn praise. Misbehavior brings punishment. And a good person accepts responsibility for both good and bad. The concept is simple. Simple, until you view the world through a business prism, where you never have to admit a wrong. You never lose, time just runs out, and "sorry" is expunged from the vocabulary. It's just business.

A little more than two years after Texas voters imposed its cap on non-economic damages in tort litigation, Alvin Berry was featured in an article in *Texas Monthly* magazine on the effects of Prop 12. Alvin is a small town guy, a straight-up Texan. John Wayne in a chemical plant. He normally voted Republican. He voted for Prop 12 because he bought the notion, promulgated by the big-money insurance companies and home builders who backed the cap, that undeserving people were getting rich on his nickel and crippling the state's economy with their outrageous demands. Never mind the fact that Texas always does better than the rest of the nation in every economic category. Don't take into consideration that in most cases, when an injured person gets a jury verdict to much media fanfare, the Texas Supreme Court strikes down that award and you never hear about that part of the story.

I wouldn't claim that everyone who voted for Prop 12 was ignorant. After all, 10 or 12 of them own insurance companies and knew perfectly well what they were doing. For the rest, "uninformed" is the better word. Key to the passage of hard-right policies is the ability to find a large-enough block of people who don't know anyone who would be affected by such changes in the law. Once you meet a grotesquely injured person with little recourse in the courts, the human factor kicks in, the part that Jesus talked about when he said we should care for the sick and homeless, the widows and orphans, those less fortunate than ourselves. We become compassionate and the case for limiting access to the courts to protect wrongdoers breaks down.

Alvin Berry didn't really know anyone who would be affected by Prop 12. He certainly never thought of himself as someone who would be involved in a lawsuit. He didn't even know that the new law he supported restricted non-economic damages to $250,000 – didn't know until a doctor failed to diagnose his prostate cancer and he tried to bring a lawsuit. An attorney informed him that he could only sue this one physician for $250,000. And it never occurred to him that because he was retired, he was considered worthless according to the new law he had voted for, because he could show no future of making money. His life – in the eyes of the judicial system – was worth $250,000 and not one penny more.

Lots of Blame to Go Around

The saga of Alvin Berry is one of many examples where the good nature and pure heart of worthwhile people, under the influence of rogue elements, has been twisted into something indescribable. That's how Enron made the news. The relatively modest gas pipeline company grew through complex transactions later determined to be illegal and then sold everyone a bill of goods written on what may as well have been magician's flash paper. One spark and it disappeared in a puff.

The list of people who bear some responsibility for creating Enron-like nightmares is long and diverse. Arthur Andersen allowed Enron tremendous freedom in a variety of accounting schemes. Andersen was eventually found guilty of destroying evidence after a binge that kept shredders running at the company's Houston office for days (and nights) on end. Federal regulators had a hand in this, approving a bizarre accounting system that allowed Enron to show paper profits by simply changing the economic forecast for a particular deal.

Then the banks participated. Some of the biggest banks in the world asked too few questions about the specifics of Enron deals guaranteed to generate profits. The company's board of directors ignored the potential for conflict of interest in agreements that allowed company officers to build outside partnerships that did business with Enron. Analysts charged with watching the company and providing key insight to investors failed. Lawyers approved papers filed with the government touting the company's success. Responsibility went out the window. The world that spawned Enron is the same one in which each of us must work, shop and survive, and the rules are far different from those of just a few decades ago. The biggest difference? Today, accolades go to those who can identify unique, creative interpretations of the law or regulations.

The Awkward Politics of Creative Legal Thinking

To view the beginnings of creative legal thinking, glance back 60 years. You'll find a vastly different nation. In the late 1940s, the U.S. was just testing its post-war muscle. The country's economic engine revved with a prosperity that washed away any remnants of the Great Depression of the 1930s. People banked on working entire professional lives with one company. And the post-war baby boom gave rise to the most identifiable social group in the nation's history.

But while many people thrived, others failed to catch the prosperity wave. The color of a person's skin could disenfranchise them, prohibit them from attending the same school as a white person, or even drink from the same water fountain. Men made more money than women for the same work because, after all, they had a family to support.

For perhaps the first time in our nation's history, we had the time, wherewithal and inclination to question a wildly unbalanced social structure. Certainly people of color, mostly in the South, decided to stand up for themselves. And the drama of social change played out in front of us. It wasn't the president or Congress that framed the issues and resolved them: it was the courts.

This was a complex time, deserving the countless books and learned articles attempting to offer explanation. For the first time, the law was viewed as a means of social change if only we could embrace creative interpretations of the law. By the 1960s, a U.S. Supreme Court overseen by Chief Justice Earl Warren would test the validity of laws meant to cure social ills against the dictates of the U.S. Constitution. Warren oversaw a series of cases that determined the power of legal creativity.

The nine justices of the Supreme Court have the power to invalidate legislation or even actions of the President. For the Warren Court, which lasted from 1953 to 1969, a broad reading of the personal freedoms in the Constitution defined a new path.

The Warren court addressed school segregation, the mapping of voting districts and safeguards for the rights of defendants in criminal trials. One case, *Brown vs. Board of Education*, explains the approach.

In weighing the issue of school segregation, Warren embraced fairness and common sense more than a dispassionate reading of the Fourteenth Amendment to the U.S. Constitution, which sets out the rights of citizenship. The Court's decisions, blurring the distinction between an absolute reading of the law versus a more interpretive approach, represented a fundamental change.

Over time, the same philosophical approach permeated the entire legal and business culture. There was room for legal creativity at all levels. And the ability to custom-fit business practices to the times fueled a post-war economic surge greater than any in the history of the world.

But in this creativity you can see the beginnings of a loose interpretation of the Constitution, what critics would come to call judicial activism. This approach was a great positive step, but it had its downside. The overall loosening of social structure allowed perfectly reasonable business practices to be transformed into something almost unheard of, and it led indirectly to robbery at pen point. With the freedom of situational ethics came a class of thieves and scoundrels who felt free to play with and outside the rules. Using methods reminiscent of snake oil salesmen, they've been able to gain a toehold in the "respectable" business community. And so you wind up with investors watching hard-earned cash evaporate due to creative accounting and interpretations of the law that help a company go from royalty to rogue almost overnight.

Like a Person Without a Soul

Whether it's General Motors or two friends who build a small business, corporations are an integral part of the economic landscape. And they have the capacity to become soulless creations, bastards of our economy capable of great fiscal good and greater individual damage.

And when it comes to the law, a multi-billion-dollar corporation carries the same legal standing as any man or woman. A corporation is an artificial person, which can sue or be sued. It can raise money by issuing stocks and sign contracts for business deals, and its liability is limited to its assets, protecting shareholders from risk. A corporation, however, lacks a soul. There is no governing morality except the law. Weakening the law reduces corporate morality by lessening consequences for bad behavior. People who might be perfectly moral as human beings can be ruthless when acting as a corporation.

The people who put money into the company are shielded from the corporation's actions. The investors' only interest is how much money the corporation can generate. In fact, corporate leaders are financially and legally bound to put the investor's interests first, and there's no legal requirement for morals or fairness. If a strategy doesn't break the law and it makes money, a corporation can embrace nearly any tactic. Just make a profit for the shareholders.

The legacy of industrial behemoths extends back into the 19th Century, when John D. Rockefeller's Standard Oil made him the richest man in America and spurred the federal government to break up a company considered to have a stranglehold on the entire country through this one vital resource.

Rockefeller showed creativity of his own with creation of the Southern Improvement Company, a scheme to unite oil-carrying railroads and refiners and tie them together to guarantee profitable pricing. The system was fraught with unfairness. For example, any non-participating refiner had to pay more to transport oil, essentially creating a tax on non-members. Breaking apart Standard Oil did little to harm Rockefeller's wealth, but it did help the United States set the boundaries for restraint of trade and monopoly.

Decades later, government leaders have again tried to ease the power intrinsic to corporations. The Sarbanes-Oxley Act of 2002 was designed to curb accounting fraud and hold company management accountable for their business's actions. This law attempted to rein in everyone from executives and investment bankers to analysts and attorneys. The law strengthened and put teeth into a range of regulations meant to keep corporations and other businesses in check.

For a time, the actions were praised. Politicians. Business leaders. Regulators. Everyone seemed ready to restore the public trust in American business. Just a few years later, though, many of those same leaders want to weaken the law's regulations.

Accounting firms such as PricewaterhouseCoopers, Deloitte & Touche, Ernst & Young and KPMG push for new protections from court damages if investors or others sue for flawed audits. Without the legal cover, a court-ordered award penalizing one of the financial behemoths might send them down the same path as Arthur Andersen and Enron.

The essential question is this: what is more important, companies pumping hundreds of millions into the economy or millions of individual investors? Who is on the side of the individual who must live among corporate giants? In today's muddied regulatory climate, the answer isn't clear.

Corporations created in the spirit of Standard Oil surround us. So do lawyers, accountants and business leaders who seek every advantage, even when that advantage runs counter to the spirit of the law. An ongoing debate rages over just how much oversight and openness should rule business. In the schools that train these corporate professionals, there is a conscious movement to institutionalize the belief that it's improper not to use every means available to help your client short of the illegal. Unethical is okay. Shades of grey represent a green light to maximize profit.

When Trying to Control Financial Criminals, It's Pay Me Now or Pay Me Later

Americans have developed a sense of entitlement that says we should get something for nothing. Our political elites pander to us, treating us like children, telling us only what we want to hear. We've just had a large helping of this bull crap during the recent election season. You see it with our approach to taxes, which is fast becoming the fourth or fifth rail of politics. Of course, no one enjoys paying taxes, but they really are, as Justice Oliver Wendell Holmes, Jr., said, "...the price we pay for a civilized society."

A long line of right-wing voices tell us we are taxed into servitude, but a comparison with other industrialized nations shows that's not true. In an annual survey of 30 countries in Europe, North America and Asia by the Organization for Economic Cooperation and Development (IECD), the U.S. ranked twenty-ninth in national and local taxes as a share of Gross Domestic Product (GDP). Total federal, state and local taxes in 2003 were 24.2% of GDP – well below the 30-country average of 36.5. The only country taxed less was Mexico.

The regulation of financial markets is another area in which we are markedly shortsighted. A vicious cycle begins after some scandal involving accountants, financial gurus and other Suits, and it goes like this:

First, ordinary people lose great big buckets of money to scoundrels and thieves.

Second, cries of outrage can be heard about the land, from the halls of Congress to the airwaves of talk radio and cable TV.

Punish the bad guys, whatever it takes. And especially in our legislative outposts, a hue and cry goes up that new laws need to be passed to deter those who might copycat those evil deeds.

Third, the new laws go into effect, followed closely by the realization that there are costs associated with these actions. A law meant to police the behavior of one group costs money in compliance by another.

Fourth, lobbyists shift into hyper-drive for their clients. Supposed think tanks, wholly owned by those clients, pump out position papers decrying the new laws and the entities they create to enforce civilized behavior on the financial crowd.

Fifth, studies by those wholly owned think tanks conclude that regulation of their industry costs government and business more money than simply blowing it off. Well duh, my kids might say, and where in your study is the cost of NOT regulating—the cost to investors, consumers and the financial markets themselves in lost confidence and reluctance to invest in the future? Let us hear such names as Bear Sterns, Fannie Mae and Freddie Mac.

Sixth, pressured by the selfish rich, masquerading as free marketeers, the powers that be pass more laws that soften the first laws and leave us open to another round of financial scullduggery.

Regulation has costs *and* benefits, but that fact is no reason to decide not to regulate. Purchasing and installing street lights costs money, but are we going to decide the cost is more oppressive than being run over at the corner? The Federal Aviation Administration has spent millions over the years developing regulations governing takeoffs and landings at our nation's airports. Do we really want to risk taking the George W. Bush philosophy to its extreme and making airport regulations voluntary?

This same cycle was at work after accounting scandals and a public angry about investments prompted Congress to create the Sarbanes-Oxley Act of 2002. William H. Donaldson, SEC chairman at the time, called the act "the most important securities legislation since the original federal securities laws of the 1930s."

Sponsored by Senator Paul Sarbanes, a Maryland Democrat, and Congressman Michael G. Oxley, an Ohio Republican, the act often called SOX passed relatively easily. Few elected lawmakers wished to seem weak in the wake of scandals such as Enron.

SOX improved financial disclosures to increase corporate responsibility and prevent accounting fraud. The act also formed the Public Company Accounting Oversight Board to watchdog auditors. SOX addresses issues such as corporate responsibility, fraud and enhanced penalties for white-collar crime. The sweeping legislation shifts the base supporting the methods on which corporations rely.

Consequences, some intended and others not, are apparent. Few lawmakers show a willingness to attack the core of the act's oversight powers, but researchers, lobbyists and some lawmakers are picking at the edges.

SOX targeted problems with the largest corporations, but critics focused on the new layers of reporting and disclosure duties that smaller companies find time-consuming and expensive to manage.

University of Georgia researchers found the act leads to larger boards of directors. Audit committees meet twice as often as before. Insurance premiums for directors and officers are more than double what they were before the act was passed. Firms pay more to board members, who now face greater scrutiny and legal exposure. Small firms paid $3.19 in director fees per $1,000 of net sales in 2004, or about 84 cents more than in 2001 and $1.21 more than in 1998.

Under SOX, going public brings new demands for accurate accounting and bigger penalties for violations.

Opponents believe SOX impedes companies from making public stock offerings, an impediment to the nation's economic vitality.

With so much at stake, attacks against SOX have grown. The Free Enterprise Fund challenged the constitutional standing of the Public Company Accounting Oversight Board created by Sarbanes-Oxley. The Fund, a backer of many conservative hot-button measures, emphasized research indicating the act has reduced the stock value of American companies by a staggering $1.4 trillion dollars. Supporters of Sarbanes-Oxley speculate that company financial officers might have cooked the books on American companies approximately equal to the amount the act has reduced the value of companies. Under this reasoning, the act might actually have brought the stock closer to what it should be without manipulation.

For awhile, politicians on both sides of the aisle expressed interest in mitigating some of SOX's regulations, particularly those hindering small businesses. With millions, even billions of dollars at stake, the debate over the benefits and faults of SOX produce all kinds of anecdotal evidence against it. But the view is different when you look at the big picture.

In the words of former Congressman Oxley, "Our goal was to restore investor confidence and the goal, I think, has been met. Clearly, investor confidence is at an all-time high (in 2007). The markets have almost doubled in that five years (after passage of SOX in 2002) and it was based on two pillars: transparency and accountability. I think in both instances, we met that challenge."

4

LEGAL MALPRACTICE: "I ONLY USE MY GUN WHEN KINDNESS FAILS."

My relationship with the legal profession is a complex one, best summed up by the Audie Murphy story at the beginning of this book.

As I said, my hero was not the troubled Audie, but the mythic defender. But there's a frustration that goes with defending the underdog, and that frustration has led to the dissatisfaction I often feel with the law.

I hate the politics of law that affect my ability to do a good job and get a good result for my client. I hate the fact that lawsuits often keep the guilty from apologizing when they want to apologize and keep the injured from forgiving when they want to forgive. But most of all I hate living in a system that promotes conflict as the most likely means of finding truth.

Ultimately, I made my peace with the practice of law by providing representation to those people with cases I genuinely believe in. Many of these were against other lawyers. It was certainly the contrarian approach, which many will tell you is true to my basic personality. Few attorneys in 1981 would sue their colleagues. My first case was against one of our premiere divorce law firms. Real estate developers at the time were offering three years free rent on a five-year lease. This particular law firm allowed itself to be tempted and left their old building for a shiny new one with several years left to pay on their original lease.

The owners of the building they left felt compelled to pursue the runaway lawyers for breaking the lease, so they quite naturally called the old-line blueblood firm I had just left to go out on my own. To the client's surprise, their go-to law firm, which had shared in their success with multi-million-dollar deals all over the state, would not represent them because they would not sue another lawyer.

I had no such problem. It seemed like a simple decision. Lawyers have no right to a "King's X" with contracts they sign. Lawyers should be held accountable in the law for promises they make the same as everyone else, if not more so. The idea of some secret brotherhood of the law repulses me. I can't stand doctors who won't testify against a bad doctor or police officers who won't ticket another officer, so lawyers shouldn't be reluctant to sue other lawyers. Professional courtesy should never outweigh the law.

I was proud that my old firm showed such respect for my ability by offering me the case, until they explained how happy they were that I would take it. They looked all over town and no one would sue another lawyer. Apparently, I was their last hope, not their first choice.

The case proceeded and I got a judgment against the professional corporation that had signed the lease. None of the lawyers had any personal liability on the lease, so they simply set up a new corporation and continued to practice law with three years free rent. The landlords had their symbolic judgment and I was baptized into my future practice: I sued lawyers.

Word spread quickly that I was the guy to hire in all kinds of situations involving lawyers as parties to litigation. Law firms would hire me when a partner left and took client files. Lawyers would hire me when their clients fired them and signed new contingent-fee contracts with other lawyers. My practice was doing fine and I was suing or defending lawyers on every kind of claim imaginable other than an outright malpractice claim. Then I decided to take the next good legal mal case that was offered.

The facts of that first case were not significantly in dispute. A real estate developer had cajoled a group of doctors into investing with him in the purchase and development of a large track of land around a lake. The plans included golf courses, luxury homes, a landing strip, millions of dollars of tax savings and incredible income for everyone involved.

The structure of the deal was simple: 10 doctors and a real estate developer, all equal partners. The day before the deal was signed, though, the developer told the lawyer to change the loan documentation and make him "non-recourse" on the multi-million dollar loan to secure the purchase. This meant the developer would not be liable to the bank if the partnership defaulted on the loan, but the doctors would. The bank didn't care, since the doctors were the money behind the loan anyway. Besides, at that point every project was flush with the promise of money to come. So the lawyer did as the developer instructed, then presented the documents to the doctors without explaining this change. Apparently he was not focusing on the fact that he also represented each of the doctors individually because of his representation of this general partnership.

Fast-forward a few years, to the mid 80's. Real estate and tax laws had changed, banks refused to complete the funding of construction loans, the FDIC took over banks left and right, and luxury real estate projects cratered. This project was no different. The bank (and later the FDIC) sued the doctors, who learned for the first time that their partner, the real estate developer who had gotten them into the deal in the first place, had no obligation to help them pay the multi-million dollar note. The doctors hired me. I sued the lawyer. The case settled, and from then on I was the guy who sued lawyers for malpractice. It seemed like a simple plan.

Looking back on that time, I was a little naive about how others in my profession would perceive me. If I took only good cases and handled them professionally, surely the lawyers I sued would recognize that a lawsuit against them was inevitable. I figured they would be grateful that the case was handled in a professional manner, as opposed to being sued by some of the other jerks who could have sued them.

About a year after that first case settled, I contacted opposing counsel and received permission to talk directly to his former client. Since he was the first lawyer I sued for malpractice, his perspective on the lawsuit I had filed against him was important. This lawyer graciously agreed that he was treated professionally and courteously, but he continued to assert the righteousness of his side: he had committed no malpractice and did not deserve to be sued. I reminded him gently of facts that suggested he made a mistake, but he refused to budge from his conviction that the lawsuit against him was out of line. He said the lawsuit subtracted 10 years from his life. I laughed nervously over the phone and he interrupted me saying, "Randy, I'm serious. You took 10 years off my life."

He was not angry and didn't threaten to get even with me; he was simply describing the impact those actions had on his life, in a way that I had never heard before. His continued protestations of innocence surprised me, in light of the fact that the case was over and it no longer mattered. Somehow, I expected him to acknowledge his mistake in the following manner:

"Yea, that wasn't real smart on my part. I made an innocent mistake, and I'll never make that mistake again."

If he couldn't admit his mistake, at least this attorney could acknowledge some ambiguity in his actions and the possibility that others might view it negatively, but he didn't. He attacked my actions, albeit politely, for having sued him in the first place. The incident taught me a valuable lesson: in lawsuits against professionals of all kinds, the other guy is never going to think he is wrong. So it never pays to go easy on him as a professional courtesy, because the moment you pull the trigger on a professional malpractice lawsuit, he is your enemy. I had done the right thing, and that was going to have to satisfy me.

But his one statement kept percolating in my brain: "You took 10 years off my life." That phone call reminded me of the Gene Hackman movie, *Class Action*, where his daughter, played by Mary Elizabeth Mastrantonio, is his opposing counsel and cross-examines this elderly engineer in court, making him look silly even though he tells the truth. After court, the daughter goes to a bar thinking over what she has done. While she nurses a drink, the bartender asks her what she does for a living. She looks at him and says, "I'm a hired killer."

To make peace with the practice of law, I made a fairly radical decision for a lawyer, not to sue another lawyer for malpractice unless I genuinely believe he or she has done something wrong. What an incredible concession that is for an attorney. One of the guiding principles of our legal system is that everyone deserves counsel, whether they are DNA guilty or innocent. That principle can cause you to represent people against lawyers in cases that might seem terribly wrong but really aren't. I wasn't going to take a case just because I thought that I could talk my way into a favorable verdict.

My practice grew as more and more people found their way to me because I would sue another member of the legal community. Legal malpractice was, however, only about half my docket. A significant number of my cases were against businessmen and women, stockbrokers, accountants and the like: people who stole with a fountain pen. My quest was to find some justification for the use of my lawyer skills in this blood sport of litigation. To this day, I continue to select cases on the basis of how much damage the other side has done. Obviously, I am not always right. Even when I am right, a judge or jury may not agree with me. But I'm aware at every moment that, as a metaphorical hired gun, I'm going to hurt someone. In a sense, I'm paid to be a hired killer.

That reminds me of the story of a grizzled old trial lawyer who kept a sign on his desk that read,

"NEVER HIRE A GUN FIGHTER BY THE BULLET."

Although this seems a little self important, I envy this lawyer for finding a slogan that captures his approach to the practice of law. Mine is a little less brash. After years of searching, I stumbled on my own slogan in the words of one of my favorite songwriters, Robert Earl Keen, Jr.:

"I ONLY USE MY GUN WHEN KINDNESS FAILS."

That quote is framed on my office wall and I try hard to practice law in accordance with it.

For Your Attorney, You Should Be #1

By law and ethics, an attorney is required to put his client on a pedestal. He can exalt no one like that, including himself. Our legal system fails without the assurance that we are working only in the best interest of our client. It's an ethical point addressed at length in law school, although not everyone draws the same boundaries.

Nowhere is the lawyer-client relationship more important than in criminal court, where a lawyer's performance can mean the difference between freedom and a hard bed behind bars. For most people, however, that's not the typical attorney/client relationship. Instead, divorce, wills, tax issues, business mergers and land purchases keep most lawyers busy. They help clients maneuver an increasingly complex world.

With potentially so much at stake with every decision, lawyers do not have free reign. They bear a fiduciary duty to the client, a legal responsibility requiring the lawyer to put the client's best interest, financial or otherwise, above their own interests.

And what's responsibility without penalties for being irresponsible? When a lawyer is paid to make decisions that can shape an individual's future, the attorney must also pay for his or her missteps, whether negligent or deliberate. Sloppy work, conflicts of interests and misleading billing practices by an attorney can torpedo a client. And, as with other professionals, you can sue a lawyer when you are wronged by one.

"It doesn't happen with wild abandon, but it does happen more than it did 50 or 60 years ago," says Michael Quinn, an adjunct professor at The University of Texas School of Law and a private practice attorney. While many attorneys don't approve of suing another, some members of the bar respect those who do, knowing that egregious errors exist in which an attorney fails a client. The threat of malpractice can serve as a deterrent.

When the Earth Moves Under the Corporate Towers

Some legal malpractice cases can rattle the upper levels of the corporate world, complete with multi-million dollar settlements. In 2005, the law firm of Sullivan & Cromwell agreed to pay $25.5 million to end a legal malpractice suit lodged by Ventas Inc., a Kentucky-based healthcare company. Ventas contended the New York firm provided faulty financial advice during a plan to spin off another company.

The claim centered on a decision to redeem bonds, which brought a $100 million penalty. Ventas contended it could have avoided the penalty by transferring $750 million in outstanding bonds to the new corporation.

While the numbers were large and rules governing the management of bonds complex, the argument was simple. The company felt Sullivan & Cromwell gave bad advice and unnecessarily cost the company millions of dollars.

Other malpractice claims are much more personal, often splitting long-lasting business partnerships. Consider a lawyer who works for years with a small business, a partnership between two friends that eventually breaks down in bankruptcy. Who does the attorney represent? Is the goal to chart the best path through bankruptcy or serve one or the other of the partners? The lawyer can land square in the middle of a poisonous environment and, depending on his or her actions, end up crossways with one partner or another. Look no further for the makings of a legal malpractice suit.

Do They Eat Their Own?

Everyone deserves protection from a professional run amok. That's the principle guiding just about every lawyer who takes on legal malpractice cases. The way I see it, I am simply a traffic cop pulling over the worst offenders. I'm not out there creating havoc by stopping those attorneys who just barely cross the legal line. Everyone makes mistakes, speeding up over the limit for a moment. But you have to take those attorneys off the street who are a menace to others. Missouri-based Bar Plan Mutual Insurance Company, a major underwriter of legal malpractice insurance coverage, finds that lawyers are more likely to sue other lawyers or serve as experts in legal malpractice suits than ever before. Similarly, the amounts of the lawsuits have also spiked. An American Bar Association study found a significant jump in claims between 2000 and 2003 that settled for more than $2 million.

While there are many explanations for this trend, few clear answers have emerged. Some experts blame unconventional legal theories that inflate claims. Others point to the rising cost of defending claims.

But higher claims don't mean more wayward lawyers. In recent years, the number of claims actually dipped, a situation leaving fewer claims but for greater amounts, according to the insurer.

During the two decades studied by the ABA, the most frequent claims came from cases involving personal injury and domestic relations, as well as trust and estate planning. These are cases where emotions can run high and financial decisions matter most.

The ABA study of malpractice claims filed between 2000 and 2003 found that 47.28% of the cases were substantive, with the lawyer making a real error. Mistakes included failure to know the law, failure to properly apply the law and failure to understand or anticipate tax consequences.

When a Relationship Goes Bad

It's doubtful that any one factor inflates the number of lawsuits against attorneys, and far more likely that they are the result of many trends. Combined with the financial stakes businesses face in navigating the regulatory world, there's a great deal of money at risk on legal decisions. The law has always been intellectually complex, but there is a greater degree of complexity now in regard to ordinary life than ever before.

And while there are instances of criminal liability, it's relatively rare for a lawyer to intentionally steal from a client. More likely, cases of legal malpractice stem from mistakes or bad judgment.

In the ABA study, the most problematic area for legal malpractice claims was plaintiff's personal injury. Personal injury can include circumstances such as auto accidents, workplace injuries or challenges to bills such as medical fees. A client might believe a lawyer's actions did not bring a fair monetary reward, or that the attorney failed to meet his or her promises. While possibly not enough to win a case, a client's anger may prove sufficient for them to challenge their former attorney's actions. Other high claims areas include real estate, family law, estate, probate, and business organizing.

The most common problems are errors of omission – a lawyer failing to file a document by a court-mandated deadline or filing a lawsuit after expiration of the statue of limitations. Or, a lawyer might file a suit on time but fail to identify an expert witness in a timely manner, forcing the court to exclude a potentially key witness from the trial. According to the ABA study, in about 23% of cases lawyers slipped up when preparing, filing or transmitting documents.

But not all mistakes involve an obvious culprit, and clients can add to their own bad result. Consider a man driving in a Lexus, his mistress as a passenger. A commercial delivery van slams into his car, totaling the Lexus and causing the man to miss two weeks of work. The delivery company disputes the fault of its driver and the resulting lawsuit lands in court.

The Lexus driver fears his wife's anger and never tells his attorney about his mistress. But weeks after the incident, and just before trial, the wife learns about the other woman anyway and files for divorce. With the jig up, the Lexus driver tells his lawyer about the other woman, but it's too late to get her testimony in the case. When Mr. Lexus loses the car wreck case, the lawyer catches the blame and the soon-to-be-divorced man with a wrecked car files a malpractice suit.

It's a common scenario of blame and responsibility. Did the attorney do enough to question the client to determine the man's honesty? Was the search for witnesses exhaustive?

One of the most common areas of dispute between lawyer and client today lies in deciding exactly whom an attorney represents. It is fundamental to our legal process that one attorney cannot represent both sides of a particular issue. A divorcing couple, a family needing help unraveling a will or one person buying land from a buddy might ask a single lawyer to streamline the paperwork for both parties. But whom does the lawyer actually represent? If the transaction goes sour, the attorney can take a hit in a malpractice suit.

Similarly, transactional lawyers with businesses depending on them to negotiate a range of deals can encounter similar quandaries. Is the corporation the client? Or, if a lawyer represents a general partnership but takes most orders from the managing partner, what allegiance does the attorney have to the other partners? This type of ambiguous relationship often leads to trouble.

5

INVESTMENT FRAUD: WITH SO MANY INVESTORS, SO MUCH MONEY TO STEAL

In the late 1800s, someone turned to one of the era's greatest financial minds and asked, "What will the market do?" Financier J.P. Morgan replied, "It will fluctuate."

And so it does, from one year to the next (even from one moment to the next). The market has suffered precipitous declines in some of those years – 1929, 1987, 2002, to name a few. But overall the market slumps one day and comes roaring back after that. Those fluctuations have been more numerous and dramatic in the past few decades because of one clear factor – there are more buyers and sellers in the market than ever before.

In J.P. Morgan's time, investors in stocks and bonds comprised a close-knit cadre of wealthy aristocrats in old-line families with intimate ties to certain industries. Most of the investor class knew each other and often had first-hand knowledge about why a particular stock was being bought or sold. A flood of new investors fueled the stock market boom of the 1920s, when investment houses began to sell securities with a small down payment and a big loan, known as buying on the margin. This was a completely new day for the markets, when millions of shares of American companies were sold with an investment as small as 10% of a stock's value. A company worth $10 billion in stock might be backed by only $1 billion in actual money. People with no possible way of paying the other 90% of the stock price, should the stock go into the tank, saw those stocks reach obscene heights at first. The law of supply and demand says that when there is a greater demand (more buyers), prices go up. With all that new value, investors easily bought and sold at a profit. The only problem arose when stocks suddenly lost value; the conventional wisdom proclaimed (as it always does in a boom cycle) that stocks NEVER lose money! The Stock Market Crash of 1929 and the resulting Great Depression showed those investors who didn't hurl themselves out of windows that markets do indeed go down, and they can take the entire world with them.

Up to this point, the markets were a free-wheeling affair in which the individual could use the system to make a fortune in a very short time. This was truly what you would call the free market. And we paid for that freedom with results that proved a disaster for almost everyone involved.

New laws were enacted in this wake, and perhaps the most important was Regulation T (Reg T) to the Securities Exchange Act of 1934. Reg T decreased the amount an investor can borrow to purchase a stock and set procedures to follow in case of a loss. Since Reg T, investors have to put down at least 50% of the stock's value to make a purchase. This regulation also protects the house (meaning the nation's financial system) by allowing brokers to begin selling off your stocks bought on the margin if they decline in value. While Reg T has brought stability to the market, it is now much more difficult to get rich quick in that same market. Here's an example why: say you purchase 2,000 shares of Corporation X on the margin at $100 per share. You nominally "own"

$200,000 worth of the stock by paying $100,000 cash and owing the remaining $100,000. If the stock continues to increase in value, everything is fine. You simply sell the stock at a profit, pay off the $100,000 you borrowed to purchase the shares and pocket the remainder. But what if Corporation X suffers a downturn or is adversely affected by hard times either in their industry or the economy at large? Any number of seemingly unrelated happenings can push the price down, and that's when you have trouble. At the first few dollars of loss per share, you are no longer in compliance with Reg T. You now owe more than 50% of the value of the stock. Your broker then asks you to deposit money into your account to cover that loss, bringing you back up to 50/50 again.

The problems begin when and if the stock takes a big plunge. If you are not able to cover the loss or the broker can't reach you, the brokerage house can simply sell your shares to cover the borrowed amount. In this instance, you have bought high and sold low, always bad for the investor. And the money from this sale isn't split between the two parties who suffer the loss – you and the investment firm. It goes directly to pay off the money you borrowed for the purchase. Investors who buy on the margin can be wiped out in a single day, losing your stock along with your original investment, and there is nothing you can do about it. Many stocks in this instance will rebound after a few days or weeks, but you will be busted. For you, this investment is history. It's all perfectly legal because the industry and government, while enticing you to purchase in the first place, decided in the end that the system was more important than the individual investor.

Even with this heightened risk, the number of investors increased through the middle part of the century. But it was not until the Reagan Era of the 1980's and the belief that the financial markets are king that the mass of Americans began real our love affair with equity ownership of American capitalism.

In 1983, about one-fifth of U.S. households held some kind of stock ownership, mostly through either pension plans or independently owned mutual funds, although an increasing number of people owned individual shares of stock. That percentage increased to a little more than one half of all households in 2005, or 91 million people. According to the survey, stock market investors tend to be middle-aged with moderate incomes and assets. The typical investor is 51, has a household income of $65,000 and household financial assets of $125,000. Most are married or live with a partner. They are college graduates and employed – and 90% are saving for retirement.

For more than one half of our nation's breadwinners, the stock market has become the national piggy bank as we embrace risk and chase returns on investment. Seventy-two percent of all investors hold equities outside of their employer plans. Among these investors, more than three quarters purchased at least some of their equities through financial advisors – mutual fund managers, wealth managers, financial planners and stockbrokers. These advisors are supposed to help us maximize growth, dividends and interest through expert guidance, not help themselves to our money. It's one great big candy store for investment criminals. Millions of us have decided to roll the dice, living with stock market fluctuations and the risk of being robbed by The Suits in return for the hope of being made wealthy by correctly choosing that one great stock. It's simply the lottery on a more acceptable level.

Retirement Ups the Ante

Many Americans feel they have no choice but to participate in the stock market, and they are probably right. How else can most of us save for retirement? Pensions once provided a retirement security net. People worked for one company for life, and the company pension plan stood as a sentry between the stock market and the needs of the individual employee.

That security began to change in the late 1970s. Companies began to dump their employee pension plans or raid them with abandon. It was, after all, the only pot of money left after they lost the company's money. They were aided in their raids on pension plans by federal bankruptcy laws. If that weren't enough, these same companies that had promised a lifetime of employment began to fire employees by the hundreds, even thousands. So much for loyalty and honesty.

As a result, people continuously retrain for different jobs all the time, working for different companies and experiencing far more ups and downs in their career paths than in generations before. Retirement analysts frighten us with predictions that seem ironic. People are concerned that they will live so long that they need millions of dollars for retirement.

This anxiety is heightened by most peoples' belief that they will never get the Social Security benefits they are paying for today. Large companies are trying to shed their pension liabilities and there's worry that the U.S. Pension Benefit Guaranty Corp., designed to bail out failed pension plans, might not keep up with companies whose plans tumble.

Businesses increasingly look for alternatives, particularly 401(k) plans, which shift some of the burden of employee retirement benefits from the company to employees and the stock market. While each plan varies, most allow an employee to contribute some pre-tax portion of his or her monthly pay, with the company often providing a match. The money is then invested, with the employee usually controlling the allocation of money in a choice of mutual funds.

The result is growing reliance on the financial markets. In 2005, retirement assets reached a record high of $14.5 trillion, accounting for one-third of all household financial assets, according to a study by the Investment Company Institute. Mutual funds accounted for $3.4 trillion in assets in 2005, split between individual retirement accounts (IRAs) and employer-sponsored accounts. Another $780 billion was held in a range of other accounts, such as those provided by life insurance companies.

More and more, individual economic well-being depends on investment markets, a situation that's likely to increase. Many plans require the individual to place trust in someone he or she has never met, including the companies and the analysts whose reporting and advice drive the market.

Understanding Volatility

In early 2000, many investors learned this hard lesson; volatility means stocks can go up, and they can also plummet downward in a short time. Buoyed by the rise of companies exploring how to turn the Internet into a moneymaker, stock values rocketed upwards as companies offered stock to investors through initial public offerings or IPOs. MP3.com, Inc., was an early darling. The company hoped to ride the wave of digital music. MP3.com offered nine million shares of stock starting at $28 per share in an IPO.

The company was only 14 months old. It had posted $1.8 million in revenue in its first 12 months. But by the end of the first day's trading, frenzied investors drove the company's total stock value to nearly $4 billion. The connection between income and worth was broken, creating the dot-com bubble we've heard so much about. With the markets exploding with similarly unbalanced stocks, the bubble eventually burst. At one point, MP3.com's stock traded for a low of $2.41 per share. The company was later sold and no longer exists.

For individual investors in 2000, the demise of the Internet's hottest run hit right in the wallet. The NASDAQ, a stock trading index heavy in technology stocks, crashed from 5,000 to 2,000. The entire economy slid into recession and many individual investors lost 50% or more of their money.

Lawsuits, anger aimed at company leaders, and allegations of mismanagement followed. Investors who lost their easy money, along with their hope of even more, wanted revenge. Times were bad and the resulting venom was palpable.

My partner, Robert Tobey, and I believe you can accurately gauge economic conditions in this country by how busy our conference room becomes. One of the first indicators of a bear market is the presence of potential clients telling us how they would like to rip the heads off their stockbrokers. As a fallback position, they talk to us about suing their brokers. Each one has a good story, and we are always hopeful that we can help. In the dot-com bust, however, even the arbitrators tired of hearing the same stories from multiple plaintiffs, and the recoveries became less and less common. As with most things, the ability of investors to gain recovery is often a matter of timing, as those who act first are usually the most rewarded.

When the economy begins to rebound and the markets again show solid gains, investors make money in the market and have few complaints. At time like these, we have fewer stock fraud clients knocking on our door and fewer stories of angst.

An Investment Lost in the Details

While individual investors seem the most likely victims of thievery, some employer plans have also been taken to the cleaners. Often teachers, police officers and other public servants depend on pensions for retirement. Well-managed plans can generate great benefits. But even those professional investment managers who run large pension funds are susceptible to undue influence and the siren call of greed.

A 2005 SEC report indicated pension consultants might steer clients to hire certain money managers based on the consultant's other business relationships. Some lawmakers have called for more oversight. For some, it's too late.

In Maryland, Nathan A. Chapman Jr. was a friend to the political elite and was considered a rising financial star. That was before a 90-month sentence in federal prison. He was accused of taking state pension money and using it to buy stock in his own companies, improperly inflating their value. When the companies tanked, the retirement system lost an investment totaling at least $5 million. A jury convicted Chapman, who admitted to falsifying documents.

Even sophisticated investors are vulnerable to such schemes. Before Dennis Herula was caught, he worked as a Rhode Island stockbroker for several wealthy clients. One problem, though. Rather than investing all of their money, he reallocated about $14.8 million to himself. His acquisitions included a classic car worth $200,000, a 13 1/2-carat diamond, homes and antiques.

Herula and Canadian Claude Lefebvre worked schemes by seeking millions of dollars for bogus investments. In Rhode Island, the pair lured a Canadian holding company to invest $12.5 million in the Brite Business Group, which was supposed to buy high-yield treasury bonds. Other investors were also sucked into the plan. Instead of buying bonds, Herula transferred the funds to a variety of accounts, including one in his wife's name. He spent most of the cash, with $8 million going to personal expenses. Herula managed to snare some big names in American business, including Joe Coors Jr., of the Colorado brewing family. Coors and a business partner invested $40 million in one Herula scheme. In the end, Herula was sentenced to 16 years in federal prison.

Know What Your Broker Does With Your Money

There are some tricks to investing. Professionals spend entire careers learning the complexities of the markets and various financial tools available. A good rule of thumb: if you don't understand the investment, don't put money in it. The act of investing in the market is fairly straightforward.

An individual investor choosing to buy a stock triggers a complex series of events. Initially, a broker is consulted and he or she works to identify the highest bid to buy and the lowest offer to sell a particular stock. The latest technology provides near instant information, an update of the action on the physical trading floors in New York and other locations.

Once an investor decides how much stock to buy and the price, the broker places the order electronically. Brokers can work from any location, linked to the exchange by computer. No matter where the order originates, it ultimately ends up on the trading floor in the hands of a broker. Specialists oversee transactions as floor brokers compete to get the best prices for their customers. Once a price is agreed upon, the transaction is recorded and processed electronically.

The investor pays his brokerage firm for the shares purchased, plus any commission charged by the broker. It's an exacting exchange based on demanding calculations. Stock values change as much on anticipation and whim as hard fact.

A company's financial reports, overseen by federal regulators, offer one guide to investing. If a company appears to be losing money, the value usually drops. Bright forecasts, as you might guess, typically raise prices. The health of entire industries is also critical. For example, the decline in technology stocks in 2000 rattled company after company in a systemic decline, like dominoes falling. Even the stocks of healthy companies went down. Similarly, the recent decline in the mortgage business has sent stocks of lenders and large homebuilders into the crapper. On the other hand, if you hold energy stocks you might imagine them continuing to rise for many years to come.

World events. National disasters. Politics. The sheik of some oil-rich emirate passes gas, causing the world oil market to go crazy. The number of factors affecting the stock market is infinite. Professionals break the data down into the finest granules of information and shysters use the same information to build a reasonable case for you to give them control of your assets.

Legitimate Opportunities Abound

Some investors use arcane systems to identify good stock buys. I remember one little old ladies' investment club that went to Wal-Mart and counted the number of cars in the parking lot. Over time, the car count (and supposedly the store's business) increased dramatically, so the ladies bought Wal-Mart stock.

It can be as simple as that: locate a company with a promising future. Buy the stock. Then wait. And do the same with many stocks in different industries, to diversify your holdings.

Other options exist, of course. Mutual fund companies pool money from many investors to buy investments such as stocks, bonds or short-term money-market instruments.

These funds are distinct in several ways. Investors purchase shares from the fund or broker. The cost of shares is determined by the net asset value of the fund, plus any fees charged by the fund. An investor can sell back (redeem) shares to the fund. There is shared risk, and most funds continually sell shares, usually stopping only when they grow too large.

Anatomy of a Scheme

With billions of dollars in play, the potential for fraud by a stockbroker is obvious. And creativity always plays a role when someone games the system to create an artificial advantage. Consider this example of a rule-breaking scheme to manipulate stocks and bilk investors of millions.

A consortium of eight stockbrokers moved from one brokerage to another and pushed a weakly-traded stock for an employment agency. The brokers bought the stock at a low price through a company operated by the group's ringleader. The ringleader doled out big bonuses, sometimes exceeding $10,000 monthly, to brokers who sold the shares at inflated prices to unsuspecting investors.

Customers attempting to dump the stock received a high-pressure sales pitch to keep the investment. Either that or the broker simply disregarded the demand to sell. This pump-and-dump scheme worked with a stock that started at $6 when it went public but fell to a couple of pennies by the end.

The game worked for nearly five years. Losses for some individual investors topped $200,000 before the brokers were caught and arrested on fraud charges.

A bond is another possible investment tool. For an example, pay attention to local governments, particularly when there's a need for new schools or other major construction projects. A city may offer a municipal bond. By purchasing a bond, an investor essentially loans money to a government entity. In return, the investor receives a promise of payback at a specific rate of interest. Muncipal bonds, or munis, offer low interest but little risk, since they are backed by the city or agency itself.

Hedge funds don't offer the same security. They are not required to register with the SEC and typically offer investments through private offerings. Hedge funds may take a more speculative approach to investing, adding to potential volatility.

Many other investment options exist, too many for someone juggling work, family and friends to track in detail. Most people work with a financial professional, who operates on detailed knowledge of the system.

Asking for Help

Preparing for retirement, or just investing a little extra cash each month, can seem daunting. Deciphering the language of price/earnings ratios, annuities, bonds and arcane corporate reports isn't far removed from an ancient shaman deriving meaning from a chance shooting star. That's why almost three fourths of all investors ask for some kind of professional advice.

A wide variety of financial advisors promise unique services meant to mitigate the ebb and flow of the markets and maximize investment. Most advisors are honest, ethical people. But as with other professions, those few bad apples can make some pretty rancid cider. Beginning on the next page are the three broad categories that describe the most-often used financial professionals:

- Registered Investment Advisors (RIA) – These are individuals or firms that get paid to give advice about investing in securities. Generally, they must register with either the SEC or their state securities agency. RIAs who manage $25 million or more in client assets generally must register with the SEC. If they manage less than $25 million, they most often register with the state where they do business. Some RIAs employ investment advisor representatives who actually work with clients. In most cases, these people must be licensed or registered with your state securities regulator to do business with you. RIAs have a fiduciary responsibility, which means they're legally bound to put the client's interests ahead of their own. They must disclose their qualifications, services, details of their compensation and any disciplinary action taken against them. Often you give such an advisor discretionary authority to make investments within certain parameters without receiving your prior approval. You don't give stockbrokers such authority. The problem with using an RIA is that structurally they often shield brokers from liability claims relating to various incorrect trading practices. RIAs are usually small companies or individuals who have few assets and can disappear quickly when investments go sour.

- Stockbrokers – Sometimes called broker-dealers, they buy, sell, or trade securities for their customers. Often these stockbrokers work for brokerage firms that provide a range of services, such as investment planning. They are the ones who actually buy and sell stocks and other financial instruments, sometimes on the instructions of Registered Investment Advisors. Brokers are registered with the SEC or a state registration agency and carry a fiduciary duty to the client. They should understand a client's financial needs and recommend suitable investments. Unlike RIAs, though, they do not have the same responsibility for up-front disclosures. Brokers most often work for large brokerage houses with deep pockets. If a broker cheats you, at least there are assets you can pursue.

- Financial Planners/Wealth Managers – These investment professionals usually offer comprehensive financial plans for a client. Services can include estate planning, tax planning, insurance and debt management. Financial planners and wealth managers are not specifically regulated, with responsibility depending on the type of service provided. For example, a planner who provides investment advice must register or be licensed as an RIA. Similarly, a planner who trades securities must register as a broker and be subject to the laws governing their behavior.

Unless you take some of the precautions we mention later in this book, the innocent act of asking for investment assistance from any of these financial people can be the start of major trouble.

6

MEDICAL MALPRACTICE: MARCUS WELBY HAS RETIRED

Mistakes happen. No matter the field, no matter the effort. But when an accountant or lawyer errs, it's rare that someone dies or suffers permanent injury. Physicians don't have the luxury of that peace of mind, not when their day-to-day duties can irrevocably change a person's ability to enjoy life. For those who must turn to the medical profession for help, there's no greater trust than that between patient and doctor. Your physician can hold your life in his or her hands.

Sometimes, however, the ties binding that trust wither and break. In today's healthcare system, doctor and patient have become more like supplier and consumer. Few doctors enjoy the system that has evolved, but circumstances have made doctors businesspeople before they are healers.

When the standard of care fails, which can happen disastrously and fatally, the aftermath can play out in a civil justice system attempting to unravel the intricacies of malpractice. The act may come from a scalpel, a missed diagnosis or simple inattentiveness, but a real robbery takes place. There is a theft of quality of life, or even life itself. And the pen wielded not by doctors but by lawmakers, medical industry power brokers and insurance companies punctuates the trail of pain and suffering.

In This Town, No One Knows You

Today, business comes first in our hospitals and physicians' offices. Crowded waiting rooms and harried physicians create a chaotic environment for the individual, who is rarely known to the staff because we are all forced to move from one physician to another, depending on our health insurance. The first thing a patient usually hears in a doctor's office is not a greeting or an inquiry about our health. More likely, the comment is more pragmatic: "I need your insurance card to verify coverage." Money comes before everything else.

"Physicians have less and less time to see more and more patients and the market factors drive good doctors to work like that," says Paula Sweeney, an expert in medical negligence litigation for Howie & Sweeney in Dallas. "You don't have Marcus Welby anymore, who knew your grandma and your parents and who delivered you."

Instead, physicians are caught in a scramble that can often create an environment that will disappoint you. "You've got a doctor that if you see him 20 times, you'll probably see him for a total of 40 minutes," Sweeney says. "You're never going to talk to him on the phone, and you'll never see him outside the office unless you are in the hospital. The personal connection to physicians is gone and that has a whole series of ramifications."

Patients no longer automatically give physicians loyalty. Patients are often angry or ill informed. It's common for someone to wait months for an appointment, spend an hour or more in a waiting room and then learn the doctor is away on an emergency or a necessary test wasn't scheduled. To the doctor's staff, your job consists of waiting for the doctor and coming back if necessary. Your time simply doesn't matter. A colleague of mine who was facing heart surgery said his cardiologist was in the examination room and out so quickly that he actually didn't have time to take his list of questions out of his pocket. He found himself—a heart patient, mind you—chasing the man down the hallway, trying to broach subjects closely akin to his mortality.

"Then you have the bean counters at the insurance companies telling the doctors what they may or may not do," Sweeney says. "The pressures on doctors have been tremendous and you're getting a lot of malpractice based on doctors not knowing their patients."

A physician might not concentrate on a patient's description of an ailment or know the patient well enough to identify significant changes in health or mental acuity. The harried world of modern medicine leaves open too many opportunities for mistakes.

Also, advancing techniques and technology offer new opportunities for trouble. "We've got drugs so powerful they can destroy tissue or kill," Sweeney says. "You've got fewer trained people providing care in hospital settings; patient care helpers who are trying to substitute for nurses because there's a nurse shortage. And doctors are frantically rushing from place to place to see 100 patients where they would've seen 20 a few years ago. We see patients dying in hospitals for no reason."

Drugs and Their Administration Can Kill

Risk follows nearly every medical procedure. Anesthesia during surgery for a nose job could go wrong. A laser eye surgery could lead to blindness. Mistakes in technique and judgment happen. I remember the story of a professional football player who went in for a routine knee operation and died on the table.

But consider one practice common to everyone admitted to the hospital: taking a dose of medication. At home, we may take too much or too little medicine without consequences, since doctors rarely entrust us to administer killer doses. At a hospital, though, the stakes are far greater, where drug regimens often depend on medical personnel administering correct dosages of high-powered medications meant to correct acute illness.

Drug errors are common during every step of the process, including procuring the drug, prescribing it, dispensing it, administering it and monitoring its impact. The most frequent problems come during prescription and administration, according to the 2006 Preventing Medication Errors report from the Institute of Medicine. When considering all possible errors, a hospital patient is subjected to an average of one medication error daily.

The report notes that the error rate varies by institution. Similarly, Sweeney says performance varies from hospital to hospital. Not all are equal, in ways that may seem counterintuitive. You would think that care in the smallest, most intimate hospitals would be very personal and among the best, but you would be wrong. Often these institutions are staffed with the least-experienced personnel and provide the poorest care.

Most of the time medications are beneficial, or at least cause no harm, but on occasion they injure the person taking them, according to the report. Some of these injuries are inevitable, resulting from the side effects of powerful drugs. Others can be prevented.

Actor Dennis Quaid testified to Congress in spring 2008 that his two-week-old newborns were mistakenly given 1,000 times the recommended amount of the blood thinner heparin, while in the hospital, because prescription bottles had confusing labeling. Their blood "basically turned to the consistency of water," causing massive bleeding, he said.

The Hard Numbers of Medical Tragedy

While the United States healthcare system can offer life-giving resources to many, there are terrible faults. In 2006, the Institute of Medicine Of The National Academies provided a hard look at the reality.

- Between 44,000 and 98,000 Americans die each year from medical errors.
- Only 55% of patients in a recent random sample of adults received recommended care, whether for prevention, to address acute episodes or to treat chronic conditions.
- Medication-related errors for hospitalized patients cost roughly $2 billion annually.
- Forty-one million uninsured Americans exhibit consistently worse clinical outcomes than the insured, and are at increased risk for dying prematurely.
- The lag between the discovery of more effective forms of treatment and incorporating them into routine patient care averages 17 years.
- Heart attacks kill 18,000 Americans annually because they did not receive preventive medications, although they were eligible.
- Medical errors kill more people per year than breast cancer, AIDS, or motor vehicle accidents.
- More than 50% of patients with diabetes, hypertension, tobacco addiction, hyperlipidemia, congestive heart failure, asthma, depression and chronic atrial fibrillation are currently managed inadequately.

Although the Quaid children survived the incident described above, the long-term effects are not yet known. Lawmakers who support the system might slough off this incident as a tragedy avoided, but try to sell that notion to anxious and exasperated parents.

While it's difficult to track the number of preventable errors dealing with medicines given in hospitals, one study estimated 380,000 annually while another calculated 450,000. Yet another study found that 530,000 prescription errors occur each year among Medicare outpatients. The committee compiling the report believed the estimates were low. When considering all the numbers, the report estimated at least 1.5 million preventable adverse drug interactions occur annually.

The studies only focused on medication. What about all of the other possible errors, misjudgments and plain sloppy work? Is there any wonder so many people turn to the court system to redress a wrong?

The Case For and Against Medical Malpractice Suits

With the medical system placing so much emphasis on the business side of patient care, are lawsuits aimed at doctors and hospitals surprising? If you (or a loved one) are injured or die as a result of an egregious error, wouldn't you want to prevent another family from a similar fate?

I'm constantly intrigued by the term "frivolous lawsuit." What is a frivolous lawsuit, anyway? Perhaps the best description I've come up with is that it's a lawsuit which potentially benefits people other than ourselves. We are a terribly hypocritical culture when it comes to lawsuits. The only really important lawsuits are those that benefit us.

In Texas, Attorney General Greg Abbott is a major backer and benefactor of the so-called tort reform or lawsuit abuse groups that treat almost all suits by individuals against companies as frivolous. And still, General Abbott is confined to a wheelchair because of a debilitating injury suffered years ago, an injury that earned him a handsome legal settlement. It's only natural that when you suffer a loss, you want those who caused this loss to compensate you. That is a basic human urge that transcends politics. But allowing that urge in others doesn't seem to be part of the package.

Armed with powerful lobbyists and backed by business interests, hospitals take refuge in the fact that they are key employment centers for many communities and that to allow such lawsuits would endanger the economic well-being of many people in those communities.

Laws governing medical negligence vary from state to state, but most medical malpractice suits follow the same path as any other civil suit. A plaintiff, the person harmed in the case or the family of someone injured, files a lawsuit against the physician, hospital or other entity deemed responsible. Legal actions take place in civil court and can land in front of a judge and jury if the two parties fail to reach a settlement.

If the plaintiff wins the case, a judge or jury may award compensatory damages, usually one of two forms. Damages awarded for economic loss include lost wages, medical bills, prescription costs and other relatively easy-to-define items. Non-economic damages, often for pain, suffering or disfigurement, are more difficult to calculate. Often, these non-economic damages result in the largest dollar amounts from a physician or hospital, particularly if a jury sees the plaintiff as a compelling victim. Controlling these awards is a long-running mission for many in medicine and insurance.

The battle began in California with the Medical Injury Compensation Reform Act of 1975, or MICRA. The act became the rallying point for tort reform.

One goal of MICRA was to reduce malpractice insurance payments paid by physicians, and one component of the plan was a cap on damages resulting from malpractice lawsuits. Proponents argue that such caps limit the possibility of frivolous claims. More than three decades after its passage, MICRA still fuels debate. Does it do enough? Has it gone too far in limiting a patient's right to sue?

Other states have followed MICRA's tracks, with legislation differing in form but targeting the same mark. For example, Arizona lawmakers have worked to raise the burden of proof required for a malpractice suit involving emergency medical care. The state's governor vetoed legislation once, but lawmakers continue to push.

The issue in Arizona is the standard of proof, which in existing law requires a preponderance of the evidence. More likely than not, when the actions of a doctor or hospital injure someone, the plaintiff pursues the case under that burden of proof. Proponents of tougher rules prefer the more onerous standard of clear and convincing evidence, a change that makes it more difficult to convince a jury in a case of medical negligence.

While hospitals, business organizations and insurers support the effort, plaintiff's attorneys believe a change in the law would prevent people from recovering legitimate damages.

Capping Medical Malpractice

Many other states that have imposed caps on medical malpractice claims used MICRA as a model. As we discussed earlier, the Texas limitation on non-economic damages to $250,000 per case or $750,000 for multiple defendants is perhaps the most aggressive use of caps.

While supporters of the plan argue the caps will reduce medical costs by limiting amounts paid out in lawsuits, this cap is the prime example of the debate happening all across the country. At loggerheads are two diametrically opposed issues – the "general good" versus the individual well-being of certain vulnerable citizens. A retiree who loses the use of a limb as a result of a surgical error, who has no income and who wouldn't qualify for much in the way of economic damages such as lost wages, can only sue for the $250,000.

Also, the Texas legislation does not consider changes in the cost of living. Thanks to inflation, a $250,000 award in 2003 represents less in real dollars each of the following years. Without a cap indexed to the cost of living, the real penalty in medical malpractice decreases annually.

Many states have discussed or embraced similar laws. Some take an aggressive approach, but others adopt more incremental steps. And while laws governing torts may focus on similar themes, no two are exactly alike.

The National Conference of State Legislatures, which considers any measures regarding medical professionals a state matter not suitable for federal regulation, tracked medical reform legislation in 2005. Thirty-one states have passed at least one law the conference identifies as medical reform.

The future of malpractice laws remains undecided, however. Not all laws tracked by the conference of state legislators favor the medical establishment. Florida passed a "patient's right to know" amendment to the state's constitution, permitting use of peer review as evidence in court. Earlier, peer review allowed other professionals to examine the practices of a physician or medical institution, sometimes leading to corrective action such as remedial education or the use of a proctor to monitor someone's work. The legal change provides a searchlight for a malpractice plaintiff seeking vital information. Also, Florida grants a right of access to records related to adverse medical incidents.

In 2006-2007, nearly every state considered some law regarding a medical issue. Some passed while others stumbled in committee and never made it to the state's governor for a signature. But in state after state, lawmakers addressed issues critical to malpractice and patient care. Nothing indicates a slowing in the trend, making tort reform and medical reforms key points every voter should follow.

In some states, consumer groups such as AARP are fighting back against the most restrictive changes, Sweeney says. "They realize elderly people have been taken out of the system in some states," she says. "If you aren't earning money, you aren't worth anything under these laws."

The political landscape will decide the future of malpractice, and it's a fight showing no signs of easing.

7

PARTNERSHIP SCAMS: THE 50-50 MISTAKE AND OTHER FINANCIAL FOLLIES

C.L. Nathanson was far more generous than she had to be. A long-time buyer for a local jewelry chain, C.L. saw a unique opportunity and she took it. The small company she had formed provided a service to insurance companies and their policyholders. When one of those policyholders lost a piece of jewelry or had it stolen, C.L. hunted down and purchased a replacement. The policyholder received a valuable service and the insurance company saved a certain percentage of the cost on each loss.

The idea was hers. She established the customer base and within a short time she was doing $50,000 in sales each month. Clearly, she needed help, and a friend who worked as a manager at a jewelry chain was willing to jump ship and take part. The women were good friends. They had been guests at each other's homes. Their children played together. They had mutual friends and contacts in the industry. Although C.L. was the creative brains behind the operation, she impulsively gave her new partner 50% of the action and together they convinced one of their jewelry wholesalers to back them financially. They were going great guns for about six months, handling jewelry purchases for several insurance adjustors and then branching out into electronics.

The situation changed one Saturday morning, when C.L. came by their locked office with her two young daughters. "I put the key in the lock and it wouldn't open," she says. "At first I thought there was something wrong with my key, but then I realized that I was locked out. I tried to get my partner on the phone, but she didn't answer. Then I got scared. I tried to check our bank accounts, but they were frozen.

"I couldn't get any money," says the single mother, "and all I could think about was that I had two kids to feed."

C.L.'s charm is that she is an excitable person, who can make others excited by her unbridled enthusiasm. That's a wonderful trait when things are going well, but this was a time of stress. She admits to being a basket case and called her corporate lawyer, who informed her that he couldn't talk to her or represent her because he also represented the other parties to the conflict.

What do you mean you can't talk to me...and what conflict?

The corporate attorney did recommend two lawyers she could call. One he knew she could get to take the case because he worked on an hourly basis. The other worked on a contingent fee basis and would have to determine if the case was worth his time. Although C.L. was hurting for money, she hired the first attorney.

"He tried to drown the other side in paper," C.L. says. "He filed motions that increased the tension we all felt but we didn't get any closer to settling the case." The last straw for her was a deposition she endured in which the opposing attorney asked her questions about her sex life and other personal things, almost anything that had nothing to do with the case. Her attorney just sat there and allowed it to happen.

I was the second attorney on her list, the one who works on a contingent fee basis. When I heard what the partner and their backer had done, I was livid. I told C.L. that they can't lock her out or freeze the bank accounts. If they wanted her out of the business – the business she started and which ran on her experience and ability – they should have discussed a buyout. They were just banking on the notion that she couldn't afford to fight them, and I told C.L. that the law didn't allow them to get away with this.

Our strategy was to sue everyone close to the partnership, including the backer's father. Since it would probably cost $40,000 to $50,000 to get to court, we wanted to force a settlement, if possible.

"Randy brought the other side to its knees, and we had a settlement offer on the table within two to three weeks," C.L. says. "He convinced me to accept their offer, although I threatened to hold it up over a metal business card holder that they still had, something that wasn't worth much. I was feeling so confident by that time that I just wanted to mess with them."

The other side wanted an agreement with C.L. that she would not compete with their company, but we would have none of that. She took her six-figure settlement and started another concern that competed until the original firm went out of business.

So what did C.L. Nathanson learn from this experience? Below are her do's and don'ts for a successful partnership.

- Do make certain the person you choose as a partner adds a skill or talent you don't possess.
- Do trust, but verify. Keep a close eye on your account books, client lists and property.
- Do make sure the business atmosphere is cordial. If things don't seem right, they probably aren't.
- Do employ the best professional help—attorneys and ac-

countants—and learn to take their advice.

- Do find the best possible role models and fashion your business after them.
- Don't create a partnership when you can have an employee. Make that person earn partnership.
- Don't make anyone a 50-50 partner. Someone has to be in charge.
- Don't give up control of bank accounts, customer lists and other important business assets.
- Don't hesitate to dissolve a partnership, if necessary.

Knowing Who to Call Partner

C.L. Nathanson isn't the first person to enter a business relationship without truly knowing a future partner. The courts are the province of bad business unions. Some people are wonderful team players, putting the greater good above their own needs. These people are great partners. Common, however, is the hard-charger who misplaces zeal for business with personal greed. There are many ways to know the motives of that other person.

Spend plenty of time discussing plans and goals, but go a few steps further and exchange resumes. Ask for personal and business references so you can check his or her track record. Run a credit check for a possible bankruptcy or bad past financial decisions. Verify key resume points such as college degree or past work experience.

Resume inflation happens all the time. Football coach George O'Leary might still coach Notre Dame if he had not fibbed on his resume. Politicians often get in trouble with their claims and wind up losing a dream job. The lesson for you? Always dig for the truth. Due diligence is a common sense thing you can do for yourself.

Every Band Breaks Up

No matter how valuable and creative a business relationship may be, most of them break up eventually. In terms of business longevity, there are quite a few Beatles and not as many Rolling Stones. Egos, recriminations and arguments get in the way, adding voltage to megawatts of resentment. This reality is particularly reliable for small businesses, where partners might spend more time together than with family as they try to ignite a startup.

A savvy businessperson isn't just one of the kids who says, "Hey, let's put on a show." From the very start, smart businesspeople plan for that eventual breakup with an elegantly crafted buy-sell agreement. Every partnership should have a buy-sell agreement that anticipates the end of the partnership by different means – the death of a partner or a partner's divorce, as well as a partnership that just ends.

Agreements can quell those fights that go to the extreme, with one partner or the other unilaterally changing the locks, hiring a guard for the front door and taking over the business. Everyone might not go to that extreme, but as you see it does happen. Changing the locks is an audacious strategy for the more aggressive partner, but it is not supported by common law, contract law or state statutes. Just plain ol' morality negates such an action. Yet it happens every day, and the most common excuse I hear is, "I did it for the good of the company."

While different law applies in every case, generally business partners owe each other a fiduciary duty to act with the utmost good faith and honesty.

The Numbers Guy

Other fiduciary relationships are just as important. Consider an accountant. Whether hired to handle personal tax matters or manage the inner workings of a company's finances, these individuals can play pivotal roles.

The most egregious acts of accountants occur when accounting responsibilities mix with the client's business. For example, an accountant might establish a company whose holdings include a business office complex, and then allow the client to lease the property.

Maneuvering through the laws governing investment and business is a Byzantine quest at best. Even plans that follow the letter of the law can be so confusing as to border on the maddening. Wal-Mart in some states has used a system that shows the possible complexities of such deals as the company takes advantage of a common tax loophole. *The Wall Street Journal* detailed the system in an investigative story.

A Wal-Mart subsidiary paid rent to a real-estate investment trust, which could claim a tax break by paying profits in dividends. This subsidiary is owned almost entirely by another Wal-Mart subsidiary, which then receives the tax-free dividends. Meanwhile, Wal-Mart, claiming a business expense, deducts the rent.

The transactions illustrate the machinations inherent in business structures used to create tax advantages. An accountant who attempts to generate personal gain while advising a business to adopt one of these plans often walks a slippery legal slope. For example, an accountant could become the owner of one of the subsidiaries, earning profits on the deal and creating a very real conflict of interest.

Audits also offer grounds for trouble. Remember, part of the responsibility of a certified public accountant is to the public. Filings with the Securities and Exchange Commission, such as a businesses' profit and loss statement, must paint an accurate picture. Investors depend on the accuracy, and willfully inflating a company's bottom line can bring serious repercussions. This was the problem that sunk Arthur Andersen in its Enron dealings. Andersen accountants were paid to audit Enron's books, but what they were auditing was business that relied on Andersen consulting services. The healthier the auditors certified Enron to be, the more consulting services they would purchase and the wealthier Andersen would become.

The most common problem accountants bring on their clients deals with tax preparation. Accountants may fail to get the best possible deduction from a legitimate tax shelter or may claim a shelter that is bogus. Some clients have sued their CPA for not making a required tax payment, hoping to force the CPA to pay for them. Recent court decisions have held tax preparers liable for penalties and interest but say the client owed the principal amount anyway.

With small business, the value of a good accountant is as critical as in a large corporation. Accountants often offer advice on investments and business strategy. But when is the accountant working as a financial advisor, which triggers a fiduciary duty, versus simply offering casual advice? Lawsuits sometimes turn on that distinction alone.

If It Looks Too Good...

Pick a profession. Choose any business category. Examples of the need for caution exist everywhere. Even something as common as test-driving a car demands care. Some dealers ask for identification before turning over the keys. With your driver's license in hand, they run a credit check on you to determine your salary and payment history. While not necessarily illegal, the practice proves again that you should assume the other party always seeks every advantage. A bit of rule bending, or breaking, is par for the course.

If something looks too good to be true, it probably is. The car dealership could send a salesperson to ride with you, but then there would be no reason to get your license number.

Never assume you know the truth of any financial matter. Verify everything, whether it's an interaction with an attorney, broker, business partner or even a car dealer. Know the law in your state. If you have an accident while driving your new car, who must pay for damages? Understand the rights available. Hopefully, by understanding the possible ways to be robbed at pen point, you can dodge the most egregious examples. The following chapters will help build your defenses and explain how to fight back. It's a winnable battle, and worth the effort.

PART TWO

BUILDING A FIREWALL: PROTECTING WHAT IS YOURS

8

THE TOO-GOOD DEAL

They say a fool and his money are soon parted. I've always objected to that adage because it pretty much puts the blame on the victim while exempting the wrongdoer who did the stealing. When it comes to money, we all play something of the fool. We hear about extraordinary returns on investment (ROI) and we decide we have to get some of that, no matter what the consequences. In our effort to give reasons for our greed, we are often subject to what former Federal Reserve Chairman Allen Greenspan called "irrational exuberance."

My own "what the %#@* was I thinking" moment happened in the late 1980s, a time when outrageous ROI seemed entirely consistent with the philosophy that greed is good. My former law partner heard of this California phenom, a kid named Barry Minkow, who started ZZZ Best ("Zee Best") Carpet Cleaning out of his garage when he was in high school and build it into a behemoth. The business started by cleaning your mother's carpets and grew into a company said to employ advanced techniques to restore buildings damaged by floods or fires.

Along the way, Minkow was the youngest person ever to float an initial public offering (IPO), raising more than $280 million to purchase his competition and expand operations. Personally, Minkow was worth about $100 million, drove a Ferrari and was profiled in the media as a golden boy who was not yet old enough to legally buy a drink in a bar.

Why would a mature, reasonable person (like myself?) entrust his money to such a comic book character? Of course, that was more than 20 years ago, and I had not seen everything I've seen today, and was not as cynical. My law partner had already bought a few shares of Zee Best and sold them at a handsome profit, so we were ready to make the leap. We each took our annual $12,000 contribution to our firm's profit-sharing plan and pushed it out onto the imaginary green felt surface of that gambler's paradise known as the NASDAQ, letting it ride on Zee Best.

Our timing couldn't have been worse. We made our purchase just before closing time one afternoon in June 1987. The next morning, less than 18 hours later, *The Wall Street Journal* ran a lengthy story about the house of cards that was Zee Best and its felonious wunderkind owner. We didn't even have the pleasure of seeing the stock move up and up, then edge downward over weeks and months. It just fell with a crash when the feds padlocked the place within a day of our investment.

The company turned out to be a classic Ponzi scheme in action. While Minkow actually made money in the carpet cleaning business, he used that money and a big slice of the IPO funds to pay his initial investors the high returns he had promised. Minkow expected to pay off the IPO investors with money from insurance restoration, but that business did not exist. Minkow had fooled auditors and bankers by setting up operations in vacant buildings at night by bribing security guards and pretending that his crews were restoring the interiors.

Minkow was eventually indicted on 54 counts of racketeering, securities fraud, embezzlement, mail fraud, tax evasion and bank fraud. He was found guilty on all charges and sentenced to 25 years in prison, five years' probation and a fine of $26 million. He served seven-and-one-half years and is now a Christian minister who investigates various scams and speaks to investor groups and writes books about how to avoid people like him.

A handful of Zee Best investors received some restitution, but my law partner and I were not among them. Our money was about the last to transfer before law enforcement arrived. In this case, last in meant never out.

Looking back on this dark chapter, I can split the blame for the loss about 70/30. The larger percentage belongs to people like Minkow, whom the judge called "a man without a conscience."

But my partner and I were the fools who were parted from our money, and we have to take the other 30% of blame. We knew better, or should have. The article that exposed the scam was not the first story on Zee Best. For months, there had been rumors about mob connections, bad loans, check kiting and fraudulent credit card charges. A few phone calls and a check of lawsuits filed against Zee Best probably would have uncovered the con job.

This was a story too good to be true. We wanted it to come true so badly that we failed to perform the due diligence we always admonish our clients to perform. Today, that due diligence is easier to accomplish. All of the facts I unearthed to refresh my memory of this episode came from googling Barry Minkow and ZZZ Best on the World Wide Web. While everything on the Web is not true, it gave me a hint of the truth and reminded me of my own insane dedication to that ridiculously high return on investment.

ROI is the mother's milk of those who rob at pen point. Outrageous and impossible returns on investment are sought after by potential investors like nothing else. They are also a dead giveaway of an offering that is most likely a scam. Investment advisors who are on the up-

and-up never guarantee anything, and if they edge dangerously close to certainty their materials are usually peppered with disclaimers that fully negate whatever promises they make elsewhere.

Many of today's investors cut their teeth on the ROI of the late 70s and early 80's, when inflation was out of hand and making high returns was the norm. In our current environment, with low inflation, certificates of deposit will earn you three or four percent a year, and a mutual fund that edges close to 10% over a five-year period is a real winner.

When an advisor promises four to six times that level of growth, investors go nuts. Financier and felon Reed Slatkin proved that all kinds of investors simply can't resist claims of an out-of-sight return.

Slatkin, a former Scientology minister and a key player in the creation of internet service provider Earthlink, defrauded investors of more than $600 million over a 15-year period. He took college savings, retirement money and money being put aside for a couple's first home from novice investors. But he also took money from a millionaire investor who sold one of his small airplanes to fund the investment, and many other supposedly wise people.

I ran across Slatkin while tuning into a syndicated television program called *American Greed*. This show is a compendium of "The Scams, The Schemes, The Broken Dreams..." that "focuses on how greed changes peoples' lives and proves people will do anything for money." It's a walk down the memory lane of robbery at pen point for those who may underestimate the size of the problem. You can find out more about *American Greed* on the web at the following address:

http://www.cnbc.com/id/18057119

You need volumes of books to discuss all of the possible tricks and dodges practiced by scammers. That's not my goal with this book. I want to help you develop strategies for defense, ways to avoid getting into trouble in the first place. The remaining chapters in this section will offer practical advice on topics such as understanding contracts and how to identify qualified professionals. But the first line of defense is understanding how to handle a deal that sounds too good, because it probably is.

The Psychology of Scofflaw and Victim

Linda Eads, an associate professor of law at the Southern Methodist University Dedman Law School, has seen, up close and personal, the people who devise ways to defraud, the methods they use and the justifications they make. Although we occasionally disagree, she is one of my favorite persons. She worked for the U.S. Department of Justice as a senior trial attorney in the Tax Division and also served as a Texas Deputy Attorney General. "I used to be amazed that so many people guilty of fraud didn't have a clear understanding of their accountability," she says.

These scofflaws are often smooth-talking people who feel they can get away with anything, and often they don't even allow themselves to understand that their actions may violate the law. "There's a 'best and the brightest mentality' that makes them feel they can get over any problem they come by," she says. "They believe they can talk their way out of anything."

Sometimes success allows people to feel they are bullet proof. A businessman who never fails may find ways of justifying every infraction, says Eads, who destroyed the notion once she had the person in court and on the stand.

"Inevitably, they would start off by giving a long speech. It was effective to let them do their pontificating," she says. "Then, I would ask, 'Now, can you answer my question?' and they'd give some long answer and when they'd finish I would say again, 'Could you just answer my question?' Sometimes the judge would get tired of it and tell them to answer. They were stunned that they couldn't talk their way around it as if they were on a Sunday talk show."

The Faraway Scam

Not every scam is done face to face. One of the more exotic scams in the past few decades is the Nigerian Money Offer. Sometimes this scam is called "Advance Fee Fraud" or "4-1-9" schemes, named after the Nigerian criminal code that fights fraud. The scams can come from other countries, mostly from Africa, and are communicated by mail or email.

The writer claims to be a high-ranking person in a foreign country, and the offer is once-in-a-lifetime. He promises you'll get a large amount of money after the transfer. To accept, all you have to do is send your bank information, business letterhead, telephone and fax numbers. Later, another letter asks for help in paying fees, bribes and attorney expenses. You lose money and you've handed over all the information needed for someone to tap your bank accounts.

The elderly are especially vulnerable to these entreaties. A warning by the retiree group AARP offers an example:

"The email from Dr. Olad Olayeni asked for help. As director of his country's engineering and project services, he wanted to transfer what remained of a 'total contract sum of $283,600,000' out of his country. He's offering to pay you 25% of the total to help him." AARP warns people not to cooperate.

The Nigerian bank scam is one of the best known of the email era. But technology has added a twist to this scheme, as the sender indicates that the money originated with an expatriate American who died in his country without an heir. The genius in this pitch is that the deceased wealthy person and you have the same last name. Email technology allows this scammer to collect emails and sort them by the last name of the person receiving it. That way, he can send the missive to everyone with that same last name, and odds are that some of the Smiths or Joneses will respond.

These African mail fraud schemes have been around for years. There have been many stories done in newspapers and shown on television to warn people about them, but they are still successful. According to AARP, thousands of elderly consumers fall prey to these scams, and the U.S. Secret Service, which investigates this type of fraud, estimates that U.S. residents lose a million dollars each day to schemes like this.

If you get spam email that you think is deceptive, forward it to spam@uce.gov. The Federal Trade Commission uses this spam to pursue law enforcement actions against people who send deceptive email.

The Desperate Loan Scam

While some scams play to the greater demons of human emotion, others take advantage of simple desperation. The Better Business Bureau has issued warnings against advance fee loan scams.

Television, newspaper or Web site advertisements guarantee loans to people with poor credit, often ending up costing victims as much as $1,000. The scam begins when someone lured by the promise of an easy loan calls a toll-free phone number listed on the ad. The person answering the phone takes a credit application and promises to send the final paperwork. The "loan officer" promises to approve a loan after the applicant pays a fee. He or she may describe the fee as the first loan payment or a payment for security or insurance. After the loan applicant transfers money to cover the fee, the loan never arrives and the applicant never recovers the cash.

Charlie Ponzi, He's Our Man

How would you like your name associated with the most virulent form of investment fraud? In the 1920s, Charles Ponzi attempted to take advantage of the differences between U.S. and foreign currencies used to buy and sell mail coupons. When Ponzi promised investors he could provide a 40% return in just 90 days, he was deluged with cash. While Ponzi paid off a few early investors with money from later investors to make the scheme look legitimate, he only purchased about $30 worth of the international mail coupons, according to a history provided by the Securities and Exchange Commission.

An offshoot of the Ponzi scheme is the pyramid scheme. Participants attempt to make money solely by recruiting newcomers with the promise of high returns in a short period of time for doing nothing more than handing over their money and getting others to do the same. Despite claims of legitimate products or services, these scammers simply use money coming in from new recruits to pay off early-stage investors. Eventually, the pyramid grows too big and collapses.

Gregory Setser tried a variation of the theme at IPIC Investments. He collected about $170 million in investments from 1,700 people, promising to buy foreign-made imports and sell them to retailers in the United States. The idea was practical enough to attract investors, but Setser never bought any product.

Like other Ponzi schemers, Setser used the money from later investors to pay off some of the first contributors such as televangelist Benny Hinn, who racked up $165,000 in profits. Eventually, the cash ran out because Setser couldn't find the increasing numbers of investors needed to keep the racket going. Setzer enjoyed a lavish life of yachts and homes, all the while taking his investors to the cleaners. Then, federal prosecutors came knocking and a jury convicted him.

Arm Yourself Against Fraud

The **SEC** believes investors can protect against falling into a scam by approaching each opportunity with clear eyes and adopting the following basic ideas:

- Be Skeptical: When you see an offer on the Internet, or any unsolicited offer, consider it a scam until you can prove it's legitimate through your own independent research.

- Consider the Source: Remember that the people touting a stock may be company insiders or paid promoters who stand to profit at your expense.

- Independently Verify Claims: Don't rely solely on claims by companies or promoters about new product developments, lucrative contracts or the company's financial health.

- Beware of High Pressure Pitches: Watch out for promoters who pressure you to buy before you have an opportunity to fully research an offer.

- Research the Company: Always ask for – and carefully read – the company's prospectus and current financial statements.

- Confirm Registration: Check the SEC's EDGAR database or your state securities regulator to make sure the company is properly registered or legally exempt from registration.

Find the Wise Investment

Compounding the threat of landing in the midst of a scam is the creativity and commitment of the scammers themselves. According to the SEC, their schemes can make any venture sound like sure-fire winners. If the media hypes one particular industry as the next great thing, expect someone to play off that buzz. A grifter might incorporate, rent office space and issue partnership stock certificates just to create a proper illusion.

Here are three prime examples you should guard against:

An oil promoter sends out announcements about a working oil field and asks for investor money to sink holes where wells are pumping right now. With the fever over high oil prices and a dwindling worldwide supply of crude, it seems like a no-lose proposition and investors crowd each other to get a piece of this action. Sure enough, the promoter hits oil and investors go wild in a "strike it rich" mentality. Then reality sets in. Along with oil comes water, and then more water and less oil. Finally there is so much more water than oil that the well doesn't pay out.

The promoter has already made his money drilling the hole, and he goes on to drill another and another. The investors have a successful well but nothing to show for it.

A film production company tells potential investors it is raising capital to produce a high-quality, low-budget family film with actors willing to sacrifice their usual high salaries for the sake of art. Claiming that the independent film market, cable television and video *stores have increased the demand for movies, investors are "guaranteed" to make their money back. According to the prospectus, investor money will be spent on production, distribution and the screenplay.*

The principal scammers are the producers and screenwriters. They take most of the money raised and use a small amount to produce a low-quality film that's not good enough to be released commercially and won't turn a profit.

Brokers of an FCC-licensed partnership tell consumers they're raising capital to acquire a communications business that can be enhanced with new technology and turned into a competitive high-tech enterprise to be sold or developed for huge profits.

The communication technology promised may be unavailable, unworkable or too costly. The partnership brokers take most of the money for themselves after they acquire low-tech businesses for consumers that would require millions of dollars more to have a chance of turning a profit.

These three stories basically describe the same scam involving a certain definition of success. Well gets drilled and oil is found. Movie is made. Company is started. No investor makes money, but the seeming success of the venture makes the investor less likely to suspect the fraud.

The bottom line is that no one should invest in these high-risk ventures unless you can afford to lose your money. If you are flush enough that you can afford to lose that much money, chances are you will have the wherewithal to find out who you are dealing with. Middle America has no business giving up hard earned money to oil promoters or movie makers or telecom start-ups. Exotic investing is the tip-off that it is a scam on the front end.

So many people want to run with the big boys that there are always more suckers. Think of this like the famous Groucho Marx line about how he would not join a club that would have him as a member. If they want your little nest egg of money, how solid could they be? Eventually, investigators might catch up with the thieves, but often it's too late for those who have already committed money.

9

UNDERSTANDING YOUR CONTRACT

You hear the refrain in legal potboilers and television courtroom dramas: "That contract's not worth the paper it's written on." There are badly written contracts and some that are perfectly crafted. Few contracts can overcome the intention of one party to get the best of the other. A contract merely offers a framework for countless daily transactions. And while the particulars are rarely as exciting as those in the latest John Grisham novel, understanding the power and limitations of a contract is fundamental to navigating a safe path through most transactions.

At its most basic, a contract is nothing more than an understanding. Someone agrees to provide goods or a service. Someone else offers payment in return. The concept dates to the English common law system on which we base our legal structure. With a few exceptions, a contract exists as a meeting of the minds, an offer and an acceptance.

Most people fail to recognize the frequency at which they enter into contracts. Consider the monthly bills: electricity, telephone, gas, water, cable television or a home security monitoring system. A company fulfills a contract to provide a service and the homeowner pays up. The contract might specify the penalty for late payments or the fine for not returning a piece of equipment.

What about a contract in its most basic form, such as someone shopping for groceries? A store provides goods and the shopper pays. Is that a contract? What happens in this case if the package of ground beef or jug of milk is spoiled? The store broke an unwritten contract to sell a safe, usable product. Similarly, what if the check paying for the groceries bounces? The shopper voided his or her portion of the deal and risks the obvious penalties.

Most contracts are more complex than the intrinsic agreement between shopper and grocer, but the point is important: everyone must cope with a contract at some point. While the specifics may change from state to state, the essential facts of negotiating our web of contracts hold true.

Unwritten Still Counts

If you think *written* contracts predominate, just try to keep track of all the *oral* contracts you make with others. You promise to do this if she promises to do that. Most contracts do not require pen and paper. Instead, agreeing to a transaction creates a contract, a formalization of the idea that someone's word is his bond.

A friend living a few houses down the street puts a for sale sign in the window of the family sedan. You spot the deal, check out the car and make an offer. The seller accepts, takes a check and hands over the keys. When your spouse arrives home, though, things go south. The family needs an SUV, not another sedan, and the color stinks. You hit the sidewalk and take the keys back, just two hours after writing the check. The seller just laughs. A deal's a deal, right? A man's word is his bond, and all that?

With everyone's position set in stone, the whole mess lands in court. You argue that no contract existed to buy the car. Nothing, after all, was on paper. The judge, though, looks at your cancelled check, which is evidence of an oral agreement. You lose the case, wind up paying the court costs of your now ticked-off neighbor and find yourself the owner of an unwanted, ugly car.

The particulars play out differently in each instance, but the basic idea is the same. A man's or woman's word really is his or her bond in most cases. Orally agreeing to a deal can create a contract, but often fine distinctions determine the viability of an agreement.

A concept known as the statute of frauds often gives law students headaches, but it's also a window into the intricacies underlying seemingly straightforward agreements.

In most states, oral contracts have time limits. Many actions stipulated in an oral contract are invalid if they cannot be performed within one calendar year. If the owner of a lawn service verbally agrees to cut a neighbor's lawn a half-dozen times between May and June in return for the neighbor helping to build a deck, the contract will likely hold up. If the lawn service owner promises to mow the grass every summer for several years, that agreement probably violates the statute of frauds because the promise cannot be performed within the allowed 12 months.

While established throughout the nation, every state determines its own specifics of the law. Limits for the validity of an oral contract might be six months or a year, and in some rare cases two years.

The real benefit of a written contract is often evidentiary – we know what the parties agreed to because they wrote it down. The absence of this written evidence often compounds the potential for disagreement over an oral contract. Disagreements can devolve into a legal equivalent of he-said-she-said, and even the presence of a witness to the original discussion may not guarantee success. A judge or jury often ends up deciding who seems the most honest during testimony, if the agreement meets the standards of a state's law and who must live up to his or her words.

No Oral Contracts for Real Estate, Securities

There are two more key exceptions to the validity of oral contracts. State laws typically do not permit a binding oral contract in real estate transactions. The law considers real property, land and buildings, too valuable to entrust to unwritten contracts. A written record must identify the specifics of each transaction. Each state provides specific guidelines, but land deals are usually recorded at the courthouse in the county where the property is located.

The added care makes sense. Imagine the disagreements that might arise without the legal requirements. When does a seemingly casual conversation about a piece of land actually constitute a sale? With high prices and long-term investments at stake, getting it all in writing offers a vital safety net.

Similarly, a written contract is usually required for the sale of securities such as stocks and bonds. The need for a written contract demonstrates the law's perception of securities transactions as deserving the highest protection under the law.

Oops, An Accidental Contract

At times, you may become entangled in a contract without intending to make any agreement. Some contracts are implied by an individual's words and deeds, when a person acts in a manner consistent with a contract, and particularly when enticing someone else to take an action. While it seems esoteric, implied contracts happen frequently.

Consider this example of a man complaining about an aging truck to a young man who is making a delivery at the man's house. The truck's owner is sick of the balky clutch and stiff ride. He tells the young man he'd sell if he "could get what I've got in the darn thing." The young man says he wants the truck and they joke about the truck going on weekend camping trips loaded with young kids. "Hey, if you've got the money, it's yours," the man says, thinking his young friend cannot raise the money. The young man, however, goes back to school, sells his car, hits his savings and shows up the following weekend with enough money to cover the man's investment in the truck.

In such a case, where someone's discussion of a willingness to sell induces someone else to take a financial action, a contract may be implied by the acts. After all, in this example the young man assumed a deal existed and he sold a vehicle in anticipation of executing an informal, but valid, contract. In any transaction, clarity remains critical. Don't make a move without understanding an agreement's exact parameters, which a written contract can define.

While the law relies on arcane concepts and finely shaded interpretations, it also offers a strong dose of fairness often displayed when someone takes actions as if a contract exists.

A homeowner hears the sound of a work crew in the backyard, shouted voices and the rumble of heavy machinery. A glance out the window shows a dismantled fence and a partially dug hole in the ground. Rather than rushing out to stop the work, the homeowner stays inside enjoying a fine Merlot wine and checking the progress each night after work. Two weeks later, water flows into the finished swimming pool and the contractor knocks on the door. "Mr. Jones, your pool is finished," he says. The homeowner replies, "I'm not Mr. Jones and I don't owe you."

Far fetched? You would be surprised. In this case, by not stopping construction, the homeowner created an implied contract. Once in court, a contested implied contract might end with both sides taking some financial responsibility. In this example, the pool company built in the wrong place. The homeowner, though, might have to pay for not stopping the work. If the pool costs $30,000 to build but raised the value of the property by $15,000, the homeowner might have to pay that lesser amount. After all, the homeowner did have a $15,000 gain.

The possible permutations of an implied contract are as diverse as all of the possible transactions occurring in daily life. Just recognize the possibility of creating an implied contract. When in doubt, seek advice from a qualified attorney.

Avoiding Contract Surprises

A signature on a contract creates responsibility. A court assumes everyone reads and understands a contract before signing, which represents a binding act. If you work with a lawyer, ask to make sure he or she read it. It seems simple, and it is. Ask anyway. If a change appears necessary, make it before reaching for a pen. Without a signature, a contract represents nothing more than wasted paper. Add a signature, though, and that pile of paper becomes legally binding and awfully difficult to overcome.

Also, leave any tendency toward trust at home before a contract signing. Never sign a contract containing blank sections, and ignore anyone who claims someone will fill out the niggling parts after you sign. A friendly salesperson at a health club might offer a "deal of the century," requiring only a signature. "Don't worry about those two or three blank spaces. They're just something the office will fill in," he says. Then when the bill shows up, the deal looks like a dog, and a whopping fee to break the agreement now fills those "don't-worry-about-'em" blank spaces. And your signature still graces the contract, which is hard to get a judge or jury to dismiss. After all, you read the contract, didn't you? Always ask for an advance copy of the contract. Then, once the deal closes, get an exact copy of the final document, the one with a nice fresh signature. With today's computers and copying machines, contracts can be changed and signatures added to the changed contract. If someone adds details later, this copy will prove the discrepancy and serve as vital evidence.

A Framework for Success

A good contract leaves no room for ambiguity, creating a roadmap not only for a transaction but also a path to reconcile any resulting disparity. The court enforces the contract as signed and as defined by laws in place in a particular state, and the clauses defining the methods for settling a disagreement merit close attention.

Every contract should include the specific remedy for someone breaching a contract: how will damages be calculated? Consider the requirement to complete the agreement. Should one party return a piece of property or goods to the original owner? If you don't get a part needed, can you only sue for your money back, or can you sue for the profit you lost when you could not complete your item on time to sell it? An attorney should craft the details to meet the specifics of each transaction, spelling out a clear outcome for the breach of a contract and providing the court with a method to remedy the broken promise.

Also, the contract should specify what court bears responsibility. Two businesses in the same town might decide to exchange goods or services, but the contract might specify that a dispute be resolved in a court located in a city far away from where one company's corporate headquarters is located. Such a clause may entitle one party to a legal benefit tied to the courts of a specific jurisdiction. The standard of evidence or limits on damages awarded can vary dramatically from state to state, and maneuvering into the most beneficial situation is a proven strategy. If you are headquartered in Florida, can you afford to sue in Montana if this goes bad?

Not all contract disputes end in court – arbitration is rapidly replacing the court system as the place to work out contract disputes. Depending on the type of contract and applicable state law, the contract may require some form of alternative dispute resolution such as mediation or arbitration to settle a failed contract. We'll discuss the risks and benefits in greater detail in a later chapter, but it's important to understand how the basic idea applies to contracts.

In mediation, someone with no attachment to the dispute agrees to sit down with both parties to the disagreement in hopes of working out a mutually acceptable compromise. Both parties typically pay a portion of the mediator's cost, but the results of mediation usually are not binding unless an agreement is reached.

Another possibility is arbitration, which can follow a failed mediation. Ratcheting up the formality, arbitration typically takes more of a courthouse approach, with both parties providing more formal arguments and evidence. Again, the cost is typically split between the two parties.

Depending on the wording of the original contract, arbitration is usually binding and denies you the right to go to court. Since this approach may eliminate the protections guaranteed by the court systems, carefully consider the possibilities before agreeing to such a clause.

Home construction is one industry that embraces alternative dispute resolution, hoping to keep arguments out of court and lower legal expenses. Going to court to settle an argument with a homeowner unhappy with the quality of kitchen cabinets or the drainage of a soggy lawn can run up legal fees and expose a company to the possibility of a costly judgment. Alternative dispute resolution typically splits the costs and focuses more on a balanced settlement.

For the consumer, however, agreeing to arbitration and relinquishing the right to go to court removes many powerful protections. In arbitration, no judge moderates the argument. A jury doesn't hear the facts. Legal protections and rules regarding witnesses, testimony and evidence may disappear.

The idea of settling a dispute without the hassles and expense of court may sound effortless, but consider the worst-case option. What if shoddy construction leaves a year-old house with a cracked foundation, leaking pipes, an ever-diminishing home value and a contractor whose lawyers argue the builder wasn't to blame? The protection offered by the courts then sounds pretty good.

Breaking a Contract

People and businesses often break contracts with little or no consequences. Often, pushing the matter into court to enforce an agreement is just too much trouble or too expensive.

Someone agrees to buy a luxury car from a dealership, leaves to secure financing and later has a change a mind. A contract may have been broken, but the dealership can still sell the car to someone else. Trying to enforce the original sale is rarely worth the hassle.

Businesses that deal directly with the public may consider that going to court to argue over a broken agreement creates unwanted risks. A business owner must determine when the harm created by a broken agreement justifies the expense and time needed to seek redress, as well as the potential for alienating customers.

Other contracts provide such complexity that one party or the other may often slip away, particularly in large business transactions. A contract might hinge on one party's ability to attain financing or meet specific goals such as a business' quarterly revenue target. Missing any such item can invalidate a contract, giving one party or the other an out. As a general rule, longer contracts offer more opportunities to escape.

Know the Other Person Signing the Contract

The most important clause in a contract is on the last page: it identifies the person on the other side. Know the person or company with whom you are making the deal, because in the end it all boils down to relationships. Never sign a contract unless you believe the other party possesses the will and ability to live up to the agreement. Without trust in the other party, no contract is iron-clad enough to make a difference. The deal may die and the legal document will only determine the nature of the funeral and how much pain you'll face along the way.

10

THE ATTORNEY SEARCH

If Howard Byrnes ever needs to hire another lawyer, he might be a little more sophisticated about his selection process.

When Byrnes needed a lawyer to help his business with a contentious legal matter, he called a trusted friend for advice. The man's photo hangs on Byrnes' office wall and an inscription to Byrnes expresses the sentiment that once bonded the two: "There is a friend who sticks closer than a brother. Thank you, Howard, for being that friend."

His friend's daughter had married a lawyer, Charles Bundren, and Byrnes looked no further when he wanted to confront the civil justice system.

For Byrnes, a mechanical engineer with more than 52 years of business experience, the issue seemed simple enough. His company produces electronic controls to manage systems such as those governing air conditioning in high-rise buildings.

A manufacturer, however, produced thousands of versions of one small part in a quality below specifications outlined in a contract with Byrnes' company. His company took a hard hit when the device failed and had to be replaced. The chore required a repair person to visit each installation.

"It was a pure liability issue," he says of the vendor's product screw-up. And Byrnes turned to the family friend he knew so well for help.

Bundren seemed confident, and then some. "I had known him for some time, as a result of him marrying my best friend's daughter," Byrnes says.

Byrnes says Bundren at the time worked for a 300-person law firm. The lawyer agreed to take the case for Byrnes' company, and nothing in the preliminary actions showed a need for concern. The case was set for trial, but Bundren was not ready, so he told Byrnes to go about business as usual, including a trip to visit a Florida-based client.

"I knew we were scheduled for trial, but he never advised me the case was actually called to trial. As a result, I went about my business of dealing with my customer," Byrnes says. "I was dumbfounded when Bundren reached me in Miami, around noon, and asked me to fly home that same day for a trial."

Meanwhile, Bundren opted to dismiss the big claim rather than go to trial unprepared, and he allowed the vendor to take a $10,000 judgment for the counterclaim filed against Byrnes for his non-payment of the last shipment of defective parts. The lawyer told Byrnes that he planned to refile the big suit against the company when he was ready. In this case, though, the law tied both the big suit and the counterclaim together, by a doctrine know to lawyers as "compulsory counterclaims." By using his dismissal tactic and letting the counterclaim go forward, Bundren let the original multi-million dollar lawsuit go right down the drain. Bundren refiled, but the case was thrown out of court.

Bundren was so determined he was right that Byrnes allowed him to charge into the appeals process. He went in succession to state district court, the state court of appeals and the state supreme court. At each point, the court rejected his arguments. Bundren then turned to the federal courts, federal appeals courts and finally the U.S. Supreme Court. None of these courts would hear the matter. Bundren's act of dismissing because he was unprepared had killed the case and his full-court press in the courts produced legal bills exceeding $750,000.

Meanwhile, Byrnes still faced the day-to-day chore of managing a business. "I was deluged with these events and very limited in being able to run my company with all these distractions," he says.

At times, he worried about the business' ongoing viability. "I began to feel that we were going through the motions with nothing definitive occurring as a result of never winning any battles in the courtroom," he says. "There were depositions after depositions, and their related cost for transcribing, et cetera. This was draining all our reserves, cash, cash flow, and assets out of the company."

As defeats mounted, Byrnes reached a daunting conclusion about the man he trusted. "This supposed family friend dragged me through all of that," Byrnes says. "I believe in his heart that he knew he couldn't win after the original dismissal."

Byrnes believes the error stemmed from the lawyer's inability to properly deal with the court schedule. Often these mistakes not only destroy a legal case but can also expose the lawyer to a malpractice claim.

Byrnes came to our firm because of our reputation in plaintiff's legal malpractice suits, and we began to prepare the case against Bundren. Besides other expenses, we had to pay $50,000 for an economic report that was critical to showing damages to Byrnes' company.

Just before we were set to go to trial, the parties met for non-binding mediation, a session overseen by an unbiased mediator charged with helping the two sides reach a satisfactory outcome. Bundren had left the big firm by this time and was represented by his own attorney. His former firm was represented by attorneys hired by the British insurance firm responsible for the law firm's malpractice insurance. "It looked like we were in the house of parliament in there," Byrnes says.

We reached an agreement, although Byrnes was troubled that an insurance company and not Bundren carried all the financial responsibility. "The ironic thing was that this guy walked away smiling like a cat," he says. "His actions and performance created the enormous fees we paid him, and he never had to repay a dime of them."

A settlement couldn't cure all, though, says Byrnes, whose friend died before the lawsuit was final. Two families, brought together by a friendship, lost a valuable relationship. "Our wives still see each other but they never say anything more than just pleasantries," Byrnes says.

The Moral and Ethical Bonds of Client and Attorney

"You want an attorney who will work in the client's best interest, placing the client's needs above his or her own," says Fred Moss, an associate professor at the Southern Methodist University Dedman Law School and a specialist in legal ethics. Our firm often consults with Professor Moss on cases. When an attorney takes on a client, he or she must vow to work with 100% zeal and undiluted loyalty to represent the client. No personal feelings or relationships can conflict with the bond between attorney and client.

The lawyer must keep the client informed and tell everything the client needs to know to make decisions. "The lawyer can't hide bad news, including information that the lawyer screwed up," Moss says.

And the attorney bears the responsibility of confidentiality, a guarantee that information exchanged with the client remains private. No one can break into the relationship to force disclosure, unless the client consents. Also, this confidentiality extends beyond the conclusion of a particular piece of business or case. Confidentiality, like Keith Richards and cockroaches, lasts forever. Does that mean a lawyer can cover for a law-breaking client, such as a businessman who decides he wishes to put in place a scheme to defraud a partner of the business' profits? Moss says that in such a case, the lawyer's duty isn't to the client but to the law. A lawyer cannot act as an agent for someone who wants to violate the law, and ignoring this can land a lawyer in a cell in the same prison as the client.

But what about an instance in which no law is broken but a client treads on shaky moral grounds, such as evicting a recent widow from rental property or writing an only child out of a will in favor of a mistress? "The lawyer can make the decision as to whether or not he wants to lend his services toward that purpose," Moss says. "The lawyer always has independent judgment."

An attorney violating the trust between attorney and client is the basic recipe for legal malpractice. Also, if an attorney fouls up the state bar can take action, including pulling the lawyer's right to practice law. The potential of sanctions that harms a lawyer's ability to earn a living offers a real threat, although lawyers do still manage to go astray.

Taking Your Case Has To Be A Business Decision

For someone searching for an attorney to represent an individual or a business, the stakes are obviously high. It's important to find an attorney with complimentary beliefs, and it's possible to find a lawyer to suit most any situation.

Some lawyers take any case capable of pumping money into the business. The financial demands of managing a law firm can ratchet up the pressure to take on a nuisance value case. The hope of a quick settlement, even when there's no particular merit to the case, can motivate a lawyer facing financial trouble.

Moss says good attorneys weave their ethical beliefs into daily decisions, such as the choice of clients and cases. "They have to have that running in the background all of the time," he says. Is a case acceptable? Is there some conflict of interest, such as a potential lawsuit against a company in which one of the law firm's other clients holds a financial stake?

For you, it comes down to a matter of trust. Will your attorney make the correct decisions? Will he or she provide the information needed for you to make good decisions? Will the attorney honestly bill for the hours worked or charge correctly for expenses?

When the Search is On

Open a phone book or search on the Internet for lawyers in a particular city. There are more than 1.1 million practicing attorneys in this country, and in each major city there are probably several hundred who could adequately handle your case. Finding the right attorney from among the many always proves a challenge, and guesswork rarely does the trick.

As with many other decisions in life, referrals from trusted friends and businesses associates typically lead to the best choices. If you know a lawyer who practices in an area different from the case you have pending, you might ask for recommendations. If a lawyer did a good job for someone else, there is the potential to do a good job for you. Hopefully, after asking as many people as possible, the same names will bubble to the surface again and again.

After identifying the select candidates, arm yourself with information. No magic formulae exist for choosing an attorney, but Martindale-Hubbell is a service that produces the most unbiased rankings. You can find out about attorneys by going to MartindaleHubbell.com or Lawyers.com. An "AV" (top) ranking with Martindale-Hubbell is about as close as you can get to the best possible recommendation. Each potential client must do the research needed to ask the right questions when interviewing an attorney.

After identifying those who seem acceptable, plan on talking to two or three top candidates.

Digging for the Dirt: Questions to Ask

As a first stop in the search, visit the Web site of the state bar association. Each association follows its own policy, with some offering more information about individual lawyers than others.

Most local and state bar associations list their members. Some include information to identify lawyers currently suspended from practice. Finding details of past suspensions, however, might prove difficult. The bar association offers a starting point, a way to begin building a profile of candidates. At worst, the bar should provide the name, address, and contact information and how long someone has practiced law.

Some states try to make the process easier by creating classifications and certifications for various legal specialties, such as tax law, family law or criminal defense. An attorney may be required to practice a certain number of years or pass a test to join a category, but don't depend too heavily on whether an attorney is board certified. The specialization helps to identify the area of a lawyer's interest, but it doesn't guarantee competence. More and more states offer such classifications, and you may find it helpful to know a lawyer's field of interest during an initial interview.

After the research, visit the lawyer's office. Some lawyers want to impress you with imposing offices in downtown high-rises or swanky offices in low-rise buildings in the most fashionable areas of town. They may drive high-dollar automobiles and live in mansions. This could mean that they are among the wealthiest and most successful attorneys in town, or that could easily be the lawyer who offices out on the interstate and drives a pickup truck. Don't be fooled by appearances. Some of the best lawyers I know who provide the finest legal services and follow-through work in a communal system, with small individual spaces and a shared receptionist. With a lawyer in these surroundings, you know that you are not paying for lavish overhead.

It's good to know in how many areas of practice the lawyer can demonstrate experience. Someone who works in one area of the law will typically do a better job in a case dependent on that expertise than someone who takes cases in several vastly different practice areas.

Often lawyers in rural or suburban areas must handle many kinds of cases to make ends meet. Too few clients exist to justify limiting to a narrow area of practice. Still, you might find the right fit from this talent pool, because the rules for finding a lawyer are flexible. A small-town lawyer understands the whims of the local judges, may eat breakfast and attend church with potential jurors, and speaks in tones and cadences familiar to the community's residents. For a jury trial, this lawyer's understanding of the local scene might trump her opponent's depth of legal knowledge. This attorney, though, might not make the correct choice for a business case. Consider tax attorneys. They may lack the same grasp of human nature as the small-town lawyer, but a good tax lawyer can quote chapter and verse from the volumes of information defining the nation's tax codes.

Paying Up, Understanding the System

Never hesitate to discuss money with a lawyer. A client usually pays an attorney for the time the professional spends on any matter that serves the client, although in the case of some civil litigation the attorney may agree to take a percentage of any settlement or award, known as a contingent fee.

Most tort-related claims, such as those involving defective products, slip and fall cases or professional liability are handled on a contingent fee basis. Today, some business and commercial litigation cases are also handled in this manner, while cases involving criminal law or divorce usually cannot be paid on a contingency.

This type of payment is "contingent" on reaching a settlement or collecting after a courtroom verdict. Lawyers who work on this basis usually take from 30% to 50% of the amount collected, often with expenses such as expert witness fees and court costs paid by the client. Be sure your contract is clear on how this contingent fee will be calculated.

Other methods of payment allowed in some jurisdictions are hourly and set fees. If you are suing someone who robs you at pen point, you may want your attorney to work on a contingent fee. This method not only assures that you will not be charged unless you collect, but if an attorney agrees to work on a contingency that usually shows confidence in your case.

In the vast majority of cases, whether a land transaction or a contract review, a lawyer bills by the hour. The attorney should explain the specifics, such as her hourly rate and the rates for paralegals or other attorneys who might assist. The client must take the time to understand the details. An initial mutual understanding can prevent the feeling that you are being nickeled and dimed by the attorney.

When payment is by the hour, an attorney might request a retainer for time and expenses. The lawyer typically holds the retainer in trust and bills against it each month. Most retainers are refundable, which is important if a case ends more quickly than expected and money remains from the retainer. There really are few hard-and-fast rules about payment. Each contract is different. Make sure to go over the specifics with your attorney.

You should also remember that the initial retainer is a beginning and probably won't cover all the costs of a complex or extended legal action. The fee agreement should address supplemental retainers throughout the case. Complex cases may require the client to supplement the retainer several times. Make sure the agreement details expenses the client is obligated to pay, such as long-distance charges, subpoena fees and photocopy and fax charges.

Many complex business cases or large-asset divorces require more than one lawyer. In the case of a startup business, one lawyer might focus on the incorporation documents, the corporate structure and contracts with suppliers. Another lawyer might work on financing for the business. Yet another might delve into issues involving the purchase or lease of business property.

The need for multiple lawyers, though, extends beyond business situations. Divorce represents a common example, particularly those involving significant assets. In such a case, one attorney might focus on the history of a 20-year marriage with three children and a spouse with an addiction problem. Another attorney might concentrate on the financial terms, conditions and history of a successful multi-million dollar business.

As a client, do your homework. Does your job require a generalist or an expert? Will the case demand the resources and expertise of an entire firm? The right solution is out there. Just spend the time to find it and be realistic about your needs.

Whether you rely on an individual lawyer or the biggest firm in town, when you are being charged on an hourly basis you should monitor the charges incurred on a regular basis. A simple case can still require a lawyer and his or her staff to compile a lot of information. Even if you don't talk to the lawyer regularly, work is probably being done on your behalf. Attorneys and paralegals at most firms record their time daily. Monthly statements inform the client about the billing charges incurred and the work that generated those charges. Clients should review monthly statements and call with any questions.

Making Your Final Choice

Describe your needs to the lawyer. Ask questions. Listen closely to the answers, and don't make a quick decision. No one factor determines the right answer – it is the feeling you get after looking at all the factors. Decide whose skills seem to match the specific needs at hand. And, most importantly, decide if this lawyer deserves a client's trust. With all the information, decide who deserves the responsibility and honor of becoming your attorney.

Understand that if he or she is working on a contingent fee basis, the decision about representation goes both ways. In a sense, you are partners in this case, for both of you have an interest in a good financial outcome. Critics of contingent fee contracts often say this arrangement causes the attorney to settle too quickly, and that is a possibility you should be on guard for. But I see it the opposite way. When our firm works on a contingent fee basis, I try to maximize the recovery because that means more money for me.

Be wary of any lawyer who sees only the good in your case. Every case has some bad facts and a good lawyer will explain them, instead of just telling you what they think you want to hear. No lawyer can promise a specific outcome, and you should avoid anyone who does. In fact, promising an outcome is an ethics violation. With the right research, though, it's possible to find a good attorney who can provide reliable information. Making a bad choice and then switching attorneys mid-course guarantees hassles, including more expenses and delays. Selecting the correct attorney for you in the first place is perhaps the best way to avoid becoming the victim of legal malpractice. It is worth your time on the front end.

11

QUALIFYING
A FINANCIAL PLANNER

Once each quarter, about the time the training classes in New York hatch a new crop of stockbrokers, financial planners and other investment advisors, I get that cold call from some young, enthusiastic graduate trainee. Whenever I am approached like this about a specific investment, I am reminded of a southern colloquialism that best describes the telephone pitch:

You are going at it bassackwards.

How in heaven's name does this voice reaching out to me on the telephone from across the country know what is a good investment for me? He doesn't know my investment profile. He doesn't know how much money I make. He doesn't know how many kids I have or what my hopes and dreams are for these children. He doesn't know my exact age. He doesn't know my plans for my career or my retirement. He only knows my name is on a list that was given to him, that I am a professional person and that I probably have the money to buy what he is selling. Now isn't that a wonderfully intimate basis on which to begin a financial relationship?

I enjoy these phone calls because they give me an opportunity to see if the training is getting better or worse, and so I lead them on to think that I might be a viable prospect. Then I test their fortitude, telling them that I sue people like them for making outrageous claims and stealing peoples' money at pen point. Most of them are so shocked at my admission that they slam down the phone in horror, but the smart ones continue the conversation, intent on getting as much information from me as I am getting from them.

If you let a financial person continue his spiel, he will want to learn all the soft details of family and future, but those will take the back seat to the hard details of how much money you have and what you will allow him to do with it. If you let this person into your life, you must strip away the veneer of relationship and gauge if this person actually does anything worthwhile for you.

This is the professional who puts your money at risk. And with so much at stake, you must vet financial planners with care to find someone to help you invest, save or otherwise use existing wealth to build more.

A qualified professional should help with many critical choices, setting realistic financial and personal goals. Develop a realistic plan and monitor progress. Assess financial health by weighing assets, liabilities, incomes, insurance, taxes, investments and estate plans.

Ethical financial managers put the investor's well-being first. Depending on the services provided, most financial experts are legally bound to put the client ahead of their own interests. These professionals bear a fiduciary duty to the client.

When is the fiduciary duty broken? Sometimes, it's as overt as a theft, a financial manager actually misappropriating money. More often, though, a lighter blow comes when a manager guides a client into an investment benefiting the professional's income more than the investor.

Potential clients often arrive in Daniel B. Moisand's Melbourne,

Florida, office disillusioned about professionals who promised to help them manage their money and did very little except spend it. Moisand, a principal in the investment firm of Spraker, Fitzgerald, Tamayo & Moisand, knows all too well the bad experiences his industry can create.

His company provides wealth management, financial planning and investment advisory services. They deal with investors who are put off by poor customer service, high-pressure sales meant to shove them toward new products and too little interaction with the financial professional.

"Too many financial advisors promise to put this great portfolio together, but it's not what you expected," he says. "The investments may have done great relative to other investments, but the level of service is poor and you only hear from them when they have something new to sell."

While many people find the process uncomfortable at the least, it's possible to navigate the financial depths with success, Moisand says. "It's just like hiring anybody else to do anything for you," he says. "It's worth it to spend the time up front to ask all of the questions until you find the right match for you."

First Ask Who Benefits

No matter what type of investment person you use, the first question to ask about a particular opportunity is how do the products promoted by the suit benefit him? If your advisor works for Equitable, you can bet that he or she will push the Equitable line of products.

"Avoid someone who isn't crystal clear about what their level of accountability is," says Moisand, a past president of the national Financial Planning Association. "Find out how they are paid. Guard against people who aren't anxious to talk about how they get paid or their relationship with other financial services companies. The clearer they are about those sorts of things, the more likely you are to have somebody who knows what he or she is doing," he says. "It's the one who says you don't have to worry, the company will pay them, that you want to avoid."

Brokers often guide customers toward investments offering the broker undisclosed incentives that only appear in the back pages of a prospectus and then with a vague description. There was a time when someone working with a specific company could only offer financial products provided by that company. Now, most companies work with an open architecture of available products, and different financial companies will motivate representatives to guide clients to products such as their proprietary mutual funds.

"At the end of the day, no matter how you slice and dice it, whatever profit the financial planner makes is going to come from you," Moisand says. "Nothing is free. If it is, you probably don't want it."

Who Can Have the Most Initials After His Name?

"In the first few conversations, you want a financial planner who asks questions about you so he understands where you're coming from, rather than telling you how smart he is or the miracle products he offers," Moisand says. "If he is focused on his own genius, or his company's products, it's a red flag. Good financial planners are more process oriented than product oriented. The product becomes evident after going through a decision making process, when it's much clearer why you're going a certain route."

Many planners specialize in working with small-business owners, or executives or retirees. Some require clients to meet minimum income and asset requirements. Others specialize in areas such as retirement, divorce or asset management. The Financial Planning Association recommends interviewing at least three planners before making a choice.

You should be at least as particular about qualifications as he or she is about yours. Some investment professionals have qualifiers after their names, such as CFP (Certified Financial Planner).

Professionals with the CFP designation usually have a four-year college degree in a finance-related area and must meet the following four criteria set by the Certified Financial Planners board. Other requirements include:

- Passage of a financial planning exam
- At least three years of financial planning-related experience
- Following the board's code of ethics
- Completion of 30 hours of continuing education every two years

While an important designation, the certification offers no guarantee of investment success. Only the CFP board, not an official regulatory body such as the SEC, governs the certification status. The board can pull certification from wayward planners and that does represent a very real penalty, but the record of organizations dedicated to promoting such certifications is pretty sketchy when it comes to regulating the behavior of individual members. That would be like the developer of an exclusive housing community telling prospective buyers that some of the people in the development make really rotten neighbors. Not likely to happen.

A call to the CFP Board (888-CFP-MARK) can confirm whether disciplinary action has been taken against a particular certified planner. You can determine if an advisor is registered or licensed by calling state regulators, or visiting the Web site of the North American Securities

Administrators Association at www.nasaa.org. Also, when researching investment advisors, check with the Investment Adviser Public Disclosure Web site maintained by the SEC: www.adviserinfo.sec.gov. Each advisor must register and the completed forms are available.

Verifying the history of anyone managing the money of others is obviously important, and that's even more so when considering your vulnerability if an investor or the investor's firm goes under. One security blanket surrounds brokerage firms that are members of the Securities Investor Protection Corporation. If a brokerage goes bankrupt, individual investors are insured for as much as $500,000, including $100,000 on cash investments. Also, some firms rely on private insurance policies to secure protection above the SIPC limits. The SIPC asks a court-appointed trustee to supervise liquidation of a failed firm's assets and handle investor claims. The SIPC does not protect against market losses.

Taking the Couch Potato Approach

The warnings and precautions mentioned above are meant by the various regulatory agencies to make you feel more secure with financial professionals whose job is to wrench investment money out of your hands. These professionals will try to convince you that they are best qualified to pick the stocks and bonds that will beat the market and make you rich, but their real task is to sell you the products their company backs and make money for themselves.

One expert who would agree is Burton Malkiel, professor of economics at Princeton and author of the classic *A Random Walk Down Wall Street*. His book, which you will never see on a broker's bookshelf, suggests that a "blindfolded monkey" could pick stocks as successfully as a professional money manager. Malkiel is one of a growing chorus of learned individuals who believe investment professionals are either harmful or unnecessary or both.

John Bogle, founder of Vanguard Investments, took these money managers to task in his book, *The Battle for the Soul of Capitalism:*

"The modern American financial system is undermining our highest social ideals, damaging investors' trust in the markets, and robbing them of trillions."

Some creative alternatives have emerged out of this criticism. Back in 1991, syndicated columnist Scott Burns invented a system of investment that he calls the Couch Potato Portfolio. As you might suspect from the name, this is primarily a passive investment system. Very passive. The key to this system is the use of indexed mutual funds and diversification. You split your investments pretty much equally between indexed stock and bond mutual funds. These are funds that spread their investment over an entire segment, and this passive approach results in much lower fees and expenses. There is no highly paid stock picker to suck up your profits.

The Couch Potato Portfolio was born out of the poor performance of actively managed mutual funds. I like to say it is Burns' way of shooting the finger to all of the financial professionals described earlier in this chapter, who often spend their time convincing you of their qualifications and using your money to little result.

Burns calculated that if you had followed the Couch Potato principals from 1973 to the end of 1990—a roller coaster ride of stock market ups and downs—your return would have been 10.29% per year, only .27% less than the return on all stocks during that time. You probably wouldn't have had that one amazing stock in your portfolio that beats all others during a particular time period. But you would have beaten the results of between 50% and 70% of all professional money managers. He updated his belief that inherent laziness pays off in the market back in 2002. His Couch Potato Portfolio showed a 10.37% annual return from 1991 to 2001, while the average balanced fund returned 9.45%. This philosophy works even in hard times. The average domestic equity fund lost 11.32% during 2001, while couch potatoes experienced only a 1.80% loss.

The only participation you have with a Couch Potato Portfolio is rebalancing the funds every six months to maintain that diversification. Burns suggests that the amount of time it takes to reset your portfolio for another six months is roughly equal to the time it takes to microwave a medium potato.

You can learn more about the Couch Potato Portfolio on the Internet or by contacting Morningstar, the publisher that tracks mutual fund performance. For most people who work and would like to save, that's about all the effort we need to make on behalf of our money.

I've been there before, worrying about whether individual stocks went up or down, learning all the ins and outs of investing and constantly calculating my net worth at every instant. It's no way to live, and most of us get really tired of it in short order.

While we all yearn for that one great stock, just like we want just one winning lottery ticket, the odds are terribly against us. I think most of us should be investment couch potatoes. You won't scale the heights with this system, but you will avoid putting your money under the control of that one little weasel who is most proficient at robbing at pen point.

Screening for Mutual Funds

Investors have made mutual funds one of the most popular tools for the less sophisticated and involved investor.

Mutual funds pool money from many people and invest in stocks, bonds, short-term money-market instruments, other securities or assets or even a combination of investments. The fund's holdings are divided into shares that are purchased by individual and institutional investors alike. In some ways, mutual funds are the 21st century equivalent of a savings bank, offering less risk than the purchase of individual stocks but less growth potential.

The question is, with more than 10,000 domestic stock funds available, how do you screen for the funds that best match your investment profile? In past years, you were pretty much at the mercy of fund salespeople and the materials they would give you.

The most important (and dangerous) of those materials is the prospectus, a full-color document designed to confuse and charm you into plunking down your hard-earned cash.

But now, with the Internet, you have many tools at your disposal to screen for just the right funds for you. The following information was taken from Harry Domash's WinningInvesting.com and several other sites that help you select funds. Most of these sites direct you to programs you can use to search out funds meeting your particular selection criteria.

Morningstar (www.morningstar.com), the service that rates mutual funds, has a program that everyone with access to the Internet can easily use. Yahoo (finance.yahoo.com) and MSN Money (moneycentral.msn.com), among other financial sites, also offer free mutual fund screening programs.

From Morningstar's homepage, select Funds and then click on Mutual Fund Screener. Start at the top of the screener menu and work through the program.

Nada to Loads

Start by selecting "No-load funds only" from the "Load Funds" dropdown menu. Loads are sales commissions used to compensate financial advisors and stockbrokers who select mutual funds for their clients. Professionals deserve to be paid for their work, but there's no point paying the fee if you are selecting funds on your own. This is the basis of the Couch Potato Portfolio mentioned in Chapter 11. Since Morningstar lists more than 7,000 no-load funds, ruling out load funds will still leave you with plenty of choices.

Minimum Purchase

Next, use the "Minimum Initial Purchase" menu to specify how much you have to invest. Usually after your first purchase, you can add to your holdings in that fund in smaller increments. Choices of initial purchase range from $500 to $10,000. Pick the amount that best suits your needs.

Star Rating

The ideal mutual fund delivers market-beating returns with minimal price swings, known as "volatility." Most analysts equate volatility to risk. Morningstar's Star rating, in essence, compares a fund's historical returns to its historical volatility. The ratings run from one to five stars, where five is best. Morningstar divides funds into categories such as technology, large value or small growth.

The funds with the highest return vs. volatility ratio in each category earn five stars. While a five-star rating doesn't guarantee future performance, it's a good starting point.

Minimize Risk

Next, use the Morningstar Risk dropdown menu to specify below average risk. Some funds achieve market-beating returns by making risky bets. But if a fund is excessively volatile, many investors bail out during the dips and, thus, aren't around to enjoy the eventual returns.

Historical Returns Important

The essence of this selection strategy is to spot funds with market beating historical returns in the hopes that they will continue their winning ways. To isolate funds with the best historical returns, use the three-year and five-year return menus and specify that average annual returns must equal or exceed the S&P 500 Index returns over those periods.

If Manager Leaves: All Bets Off

Mutual fund prospectuses attempt to impress you with the experience and wisdom of their fund managers. But the performance of the fund and its manager is meaningless if the fund manager responsible for the results is no longer on the job. Use the Manager Tenure dropdown menu to specify a five-year minimum tenure.

Returns and Risk Count Most

Click the "Show Results" button to see the list of qualifying funds. There will be many funds that meet your requirements. Use the View menu at the top to switch to the Performance view, which shows each fund's returns over a variety of timeframes. Click on the five-year return heading to sort the list with the funds recording the best five-year average annual returns at the top. If returns are more important to you than risk, the funds with the highest five-year returns are your best bets.

The Performance view also lists Morningstar's risk rating for each fund. If you are risk averse, stick to funds with "low" risk ratings.

Beware of Wrong Funds

One caveat—Morningstar's screen listed some funds, labeled "Load Waived," that are really load funds and are available only through financial advisors. However, some of those funds are also available in no-load versions, albeit with higher expense ratios, and thus slightly lower returns. You can find them by placing the fund name in Morningstar's quote box (then hit Enter). For instance, the Federated Kaufmann fund turned up by the screen was labeled "load waived," but the Federated Kaufmann K fund is a no-load fund available through discount brokers.

The more you know about a fund, the better your results. Consider the funds turned up by this screen as candidates for further research, not a buy list. Continue your search for the perfect mutual fund for you and your investment objectives.

12

CHOOSING AN ACCOUNTANT

A normal accountant is like a guard dog;
a forensic accountant is like a bloodhound;
an internal auditor is like a seeing eye dog.

D. Larry Crumbley
Louisiana State University

Larry Crumbley thinks of accountancy as a glamour job. As the KPMG Peat Marwick Professor of Accounting at LSU, Crumbley eschews the nerd image so common to his profession. For his students, he dons a fedora and trench coat to assume the persona of a super sleuth determined to seek out the truth in the numbers and reveal them to the world (or the IRS). Either this man has a screw loose or he has hit upon the great importance of his life's work.

It's certainly true that in the new millennium, no one's reputation has taken a greater hit—with the possible exception of Iraqi dictators—than accountants. The scullduggery associated with names like Tyco, World Com and Enron would have produced little financial devastation if accountants had simply done their jobs.

Arthur Andersen, once the largest U.S. accounting firm, collapsed after it was convicted of obstruction of justice for shredding documents in the Enron case. PricewaterhouseCoopers promised in full-page newspaper ads to "ask the tough questions and tackle the tough issues" after coming under attack for its auditors' approval of aggressive accounting procedures employed at Tyco and other large corporations.

In a real sense, accountants are keepers of the keys to financial stability for businesses and those who invest in them. They certify what accounting methods are on the up-and-up, and their reach is impressive. They used to be the most trusted (if boring) professionals. That has changed, big time.

For instance, when Andersen admitted shredding Enron documents, it had a negative effect on the stock values of 284 other Andersen clients that are part of the Standard & Poor's 1500 index. Two-thirds of those stocks fell on the day of the announcement as investors worldwide questioned the validity of financial statements audited by Andersen. During that time, the stocks of those companies dropped on average 2.05% and lost more than $37 million in market value.

Matching the Person With the Task

As Professor Crumbley alluded to at the beginning of this chapter, accountants can handle many different duties and provide a range of services. Most people only visit an accountant once a year, around tax time. For small business owners, an accountant can work as a guide in charting a successful route through the financial world. With corporations, accountants handle a full range of duties, often filling vital roles fraught with public accountability. Individual taxpayers often seek the approval of accountants for investment vehicles that will help them shelter income.

"If a business only wants someone to oversee compliance with regulatory guidelines, hire the cheapest accountant or accounting firm available," says Ken Travis, a principal at Travis Wolff and Associates in Dallas. "If you recognize that the value of an accountant lies in an exchange of ideas and the accuracy of the professional's advice, though, spend the time to seek the best solution." You want an accountant who is determined to keep you out of trouble with the IRS, your investors and your business partners.

Often you can find this accountant by contacting friends and other professionals in your field. What accountant or accounting firm has the best reputation? Who filed essential forms on time and warned you about the efficacy of an investment? You want an accountant who will tell you "No," so that you can decide if factors warrant going against his or her advice. While a trail of satisfied clients marks the path to the best accountant, go the extra step and answer the other questions.

What type of business relationship do you prefer? For some situations, a small firm or sole practitioner might offer the right mix of face-to-face contact and professional knowledge. For a mid-size or larger business, a similarly sized accounting firm might make the most sense. If working with a larger firm, always make sure to understand who will handle the account. Will junior staffers do most of the work, while senior accountants buy lunch? At the big firms, you may never really know who is working on your account, as it is shuttled back and forth among the young accountants who come and go in the firm, like so many shark teeth: one leaves and another one grows in right behind.

Go into specifics about the specialization of an accountant or an accounting firm. Ask for examples. Who are their existing clients? Do they have relationships with other firms that can help on specialized tasks? Take the time to understand your needs and then find the accounting solution that fits.

Never fear asking how the accountant bills. After discussing the range of services you need, ask what fees you can expect. What reimbursement will they seek for expenses, and what expenses qualify. How much work will the accountant do before billing? Will a brief phone conversation equal a full hour in billing? Answers to these questions will not only help you understand the business relationship, but also help you decide if you want to work with a particular accountant.

Ken Travis believes that most businesses need more than someone to simply handle audits and financial reporting. "What business owners should do more than anything is have a system for decision making," he says. "They should rely on an accountant to be more than a bookkeeper and compliance office, and choose someone instead who can design systems to make the business run better. Then, you're getting something valuable."

Financial Watchdogs

In the United States, where investors depend on companies to provide valid financial information, the system hinges on the ability and integrity of those carrying the designation of Certified Public Accountant. CPAs are the linchpin of a regulated financial environment. Each state's board of accountancy sets specific guidelines for achieving this designation.

To become a CPA, a professional must complete an accounting education and attain a specific amount of work experience in public accounting. Applicants also take the Certified Public Accountant's exam, which covers a range of topics: auditing, financial accounting and reporting, regulation and business environment and concepts.

Many accountants seek even greater distinction. Organizations such as the American Institute of Certified Public Accountants offer accreditation, requiring members to follow accepted guidelines and meet detailed standards. Members must agree to follow the group's code of professional conduct.

The AICPA also investigates instances of someone breaching the standards. Violations can result in confidential disciplinary action, or suspension or revocation of membership rights. But they can't remove the CPA designation. State regulatory agencies can enforce their own discipline, including removing an accountant's license to practice, but whether they actually perform this function differs from state to state.

CPAs provide a range of services for both individuals and businesses. Possibly best known for their tax duties, accountants can also serve as business consultants, financial planners and financial advisors. At the corporate level, accounting duties may range from tracking day-to-day business dealings to service as chief financial officers responsible for a company's overall financial health.

Accounting should provide that buzzword, "transparency." It's interesting that transparency used to be a pejorative, meaning you could see right through them, shallow, vacant. Today it means that you can see everything that is going on, that you are keeping things in the great wide open. It should only be so easy.

13

SELECTING MEDICAL PROFESSIONALS

Larry Upshaw was in a sorry state for a guy his age. Extreme pain radiated out from his chest, making the 45-year-old book publisher unable to climb the short run of stairs leading from the parking garage to his office. (Full disclosure – *Upshaw is the publisher of this book. This incident happened to him in 1992.*)

His internist scheduled him for an angiogram, but the hospital's cardiologist thought it was a waste of time. "Do you smoke?" the doctor asked. Upshaw never had. "Then you don't have heart disease," he said. The patient was in decent shape. The stress test confirmed that but didn't tell why he was so winded.

"In fact," said the doctor, "I'll bet you a hundred dollars that you don't have heart disease. I've never had someone your age with heart disease who wasn't a smoker."

And he believed that until the pictures told otherwise. "Oops," he was heard saying. "Guess there's a first time for everything."

There in the semi-darkness of the cath lab were five very clogged arteries snaking across the screen. But Upshaw was skeptical about the need for bypass surgery and there was something about the cardiac surgeon his internist brought into room that bothered him. Most hospitals offer privileges to a number of doctors in the same specialty, but this was a small hospital. In cases like this, they usually recommend the same heart surgeon for everyone who uses the hospital.

Most people just nod and agree with what the doctor says. But this patient worked with doctors in his business. While he had great respect for their abilities, they were not gods to him. Flat on his back in bed, he discussed the proposed operation with his wife as the nurse milled about his room.

"A second opinion can't hurt a thing," Upshaw said. "I have the time." His wife agreed and made plans to contact some people they knew with more access to medical personnel.

Then the nurse spoke up. She was a prim woman who looked quite young but had many years of experience in this and other local cardiac units.

"I would look at other surgeons," she said, obviously imparting information that could get her into trouble. "Some of the others have better outcomes." It wasn't that more people died under the care of this team, she explained, but she knew that some other teams got people out of the hospital quicker and with less pain. They were back at work quicker and lived out their lives better. This was valuable information from a source not always available to the average patient.

And so they followed this advice to a second opinion and hired a surgeon who practiced at another hospital but could come in and handle this delicate operation. Upshaw recalls that after the decision was made and he was lying in his bed awaiting surgery that could take his life or give him many productive years to come, the passed-over surgeon came in to express his disdain for "patients who want to cause trouble."

"Here I was almost terminally sick," Upshaw said, "and this guy wanted to argue with me about his qualifications. I was amazed at his audacity. This is a free country and I had the right to select the person I would allow to cut on me."

Sometimes you have to use extreme methods to get the care you want and need. Luckily, most medical situations are not emergencies. Sometimes you have days or weeks to perform your due diligence. As we have seen, a little work on the front end can smooth the process and create a better result. Too often, though, people rely more on faith than research when choosing a hospital or physician.

"For some reason, we suspend the rules that apply to everything else when it comes to medicine," says Paula Sweeney, an attorney who is an expert in medical negligence litigation. "If you are going to buy a car, you research it. You go to *Consumer Reports* and ask people about it. But for some reason, when it comes to medicine, people make haphazard decisions. They are afraid to ask questions."

The habit of relying more on faith than practicality rarely stops with physicians. Even when deciding what hospital to use, too many people place a greater emphasis on convenience than on medical care.

For malpractice lawyers such as Sweeney, the stakes are clear. Her phones ring with calls from people seeking legal help after treatment in a hospital. Sweeney says she often knows what happened as soon as a potential client mentions a certain hospital and a procedure, although the public rarely knows the scuttlebutt of each hospital or specific doctors. "Lawyers who do malpractice know what the reputations are, but it's almost impossible for the consuming public to find that out," she says.

A Decision for Health

Some rules typically apply when choosing a hospital, and usually larger, better established medical centers in major cities, as well as teaching hospitals, offer patients the best odds of successful outcomes. Generally, the better hospitals attract the highest-performing physicians. A doctor can open his or her own practice, but hospitals must grant a doctor the privilege of practicing and use of the hospital's resources. This offers a measure of accountability, allowing a rudimentary vetting of physicians by hospitals.

"The guys who get busted out of the big hospitals or at the teaching hospitals tend to end up at the bum little hospitals," Sweeney says. Mistakes can happen anywhere, but she believes the odds of avoiding a medical error or surviving a mishap are better at major hospitals.

Taking Responsibility for Your Own Care

Searching for a physician carries a similar test. No universal guide points the way, but research and common sense can make a difference. The way to find a good specialist is to question your internist, asking who performs best for a given treatment or diagnostic need. Collect the names and then start digging deeper.

The results may largely depend on where you live. Physicians carry protections unlike those of any other professional field. Tracking a doctor's professional history, such as any sanctions or lawsuits, can prove difficult. Even after a lawsuit, confidentiality clauses in settlement agreements can make specifics difficult to glean. An injured patient might even default on a monetary settlement for going public. Most states have a medical board that is supposed to oversee doctors. Massachusetts was one of the first states to tell about lawsuits or the history of complaints filed against a physician. In other states, skimpy records make it difficult to learn much more than if a doctor has a license to practice, or if the license is suspended. While results may vary from state to state, take the time to check and know the rules in your area.

When it comes right down to it, patients today are in charge of managing their own care, and many of us spend hours on the Internet researching medical topics so we can go to medical appointments armed with facts. Younger physicians often welcome the trend, although older doctors accustomed to complacent, less-informed patients often find it disconcerting.

Of course, there is a fine line between informed and obsessive. My daughter, for instance, may be on the obsessive side of the line: she rarely goes to the doctor without cataloguing the various diseases that could possibly be afflicting her.

That being said, most people who take the time to educate themselves make better partners in a healthcare system increasingly requiring doctors and patients to work together to decide treatment plans and navigate insurance requirements. This can serve as a shortcut during treatment, allowing the doctor to address your specific questions without having to restate the basics. Informed consent to treatment is what you want to be able to give the doctor and other hospital personnel. An informed patient, though, does not replace a physician's responsibility for making correct medical decisions.

As a patient, you should track every step of the treatment, every payment to the hospital and every correspondence. "You need to use the same process that you already use," Sweeney says. "If you're a file keeper, keep a file. If you're a diary writer, keep a diary. People need to manage their medical affairs the way they manage their ordinary affairs. For some reason, people just don't do that."

When a Doctor Becomes an Entrepreneur

Because of complexity in the health insurance system and shifts in government policies toward medical care, the business of being a physician can be more trying than the medical part. Many doctors create one-stop medical centers combining complementary disciplines. Specialists in orthopedic care or sports medicine might team with a physical therapy group, putting all their services under one roof. Other doctors have sought new ways of making money, opening businesses such as magnetic resonance imaging (MRI) centers that generate big profits.

Development of doctor-owned hospitals designed to provide high-quality care and specialty services is one controversial trend. Critics fear such hospitals will undercut taxpayer-supported community hospitals, which must provide services such as emergency care.

About 130 doctor-owned hospitals operate in the nation, with many more being planned. There is new interest in developing these hospitals, potentially further blurring the line between a physician's responsibility to patients and his or her business.

As a patient, you should be skeptical about those relationships. Do you think it's really coincidental that a doctor who owns a series of MRI centers would prescribe that test more than other doctors?

Never hesitate to ask about the relationships a doctor has with other businesses. The existence of these relationships is not illegal or unethical. You just need to know about them. Legally, a physician must not hide the information. Massachusetts has investigated physicians improperly referring patients to MRI centers and lawmakers have discussed ways to prevent conflicts of interest. "You can't be like a little kid being led around," Sweeney says. "You have to take some responsibility for your own care."

14

Grand Deception: The Marketing of Professional Services

In 1977, the United States Supreme Court recognized lawyers' constitutional right to advertise their services. Lawyer jokes soon followed.

This excerpt from a recent intensive study of lawyer marketing trends done at Georgetown Law School emphasizes the great change that took place in the public perception of lawyers after they began to advertise. It wasn't so much that advertising itself was so laughable in those early days, but rather the quality of the ads themselves. You've seen them if you ever stayed home from work, sick with the flu, watching daytime TV. An attorney with little on-air preparation is yelling at the camera, promising recovery. He has a name like The Iron Fist or is walking a pit bull. The clients in the spot are not just victims. Around their necks are special effects numbers, like necklaces, that tell how much the attorney won for them.

Of course, if this scene was entirely in the service of people seeking legal services, you would have a split screen with half of the picture devoted to two figures on the golf course—the general counsel of one of the companies being sued and defense counsel wanting his business—planning how they might deprive consumers of justice in the courts. State bar associations all across the country have erected as many roadblocks as possible against the marketing of legal services by plaintiff's attorneys, while manipulation on the corporate side is "just business."

Just as long as attorneys have been allowed to advertise, that's how long lawyer groups have been trying to restrict them. Because some individual attorneys can be extremely creative, this has caused the advertising to be more so and has expanded the definition of attorney marketing.

For instance, I learned of one criminal attorney who made his living representing people charged with such offenses as driving while intoxicated, domestic violence and snatch 'n grab robbery. By noon each day, this attorney had a list of the names and addresses of those people who had bailed out of jail on these offenses the night before. His marketing consisted of sending letters and simple brochures to the people charged, offering his services on their behalf. Of course, many other attorneys had the same list, and our man wanted to make sure his mailer stood out and increased the number of those accused of minor offenses that he would sign up for representation. That's when he asked a marketing consultant to design a mailer that looked exactly like an official court summons for his state and county. This mailer would include an official-looking state seal and verbiage giving the impression that the accused person was being officially summoned by the court to come to the attorney's office and hire him.

The consultant, who worked for a number of law firms, told the attorney that his request was unethical for both of them and was probably illegal for the attorney under his state's rules of professional conduct. He declined the work but knew that the attorney had this mailer created elsewhere. It was not long afterword that the attorney was disbarred for a number of violations.

As attorneys push the edge of the marketing envelope, bar associations work to enact a number of restrictions. Some states have tried to outlaw lawyer advertising on the state level, but court challenges nixed those efforts. Other states began to require disclaimers on the advertising, and many of those still stand. I'm especially amused at the disclaimer required in Alabama, which says:

"No representation is made that the quality of the legal services to be performed is greater than the quality of legal services performed by other lawyers."

What this statement says is that we have produced this quality television commercial, sent you this four-color brochure or poured out our hearts for page after page of our firm Web site, but pay no attention to that. According to bar rules, we aren't one bit better than the next lawyer.

Professional Duty the Difference

Because lawyers carry a fiduciary responsibility, protecting a client's best interest above all else, over-promising results and inflating professional experience can weaken the client-attorney trust. Legal professionals are not alone. Physicians and financial professionals bear similar concerns. Each carries a unique responsibility to clients, who depend on the honesty and professionalism of experts in fields that can shape a person's health and financial well-being.

But we live in a hyper-marketed world filled with the chatter of advertisers, seemingly screaming a message from every available public space and electronic device. Even personal interactions fall into the trap, such as those defense-side attorneys playing golf, attending dinner parties or donating at fundraisers. Isn't networking the most intimate form of marketing?

For lawyers, the move toward modern marketing happened at a glacial pace until the Internet became the place to advertise. Buzzwords such as branding and image advertising have certainly crept into the lingo, but in most large firms there are usually only a handful of attorneys who embrace these concepts and many who are still mystified by them. Others, particularly new lawyers or small firms, want to entice you to pay attention to them. The arbiter of propriety in attorney advertising and marketing is the American Bar Association's Model Rules for Professional Conduct.

The rules govern more than just television ads or marketing brochures, drawing broad guidelines that set the tone for the client-attorney relationship. Any contact with potential clients falls under these rules. Each state may set additional guidelines, such as curbs on overly aggressive ads or limitations on access to some police files used to identify crime victims who could become potential clients.

Several states have established advertising review procedures that regulate how lawyers in that state reach out to possible clients. One area of focus is ads that create unjustified expectations, including prohibiting claims that a lawyer or firm has been more successful than competitors in achieving results for clients without facts to back up the claim. And the lawyer or firm doing the advertising must provide the details to the commission.

While each state may set its own rules and regulatory system for attorneys, the ABA's guidelines provide a foundation.

The first ABA rule prohibits a lawyer from making a false or misleading communication about his or her services, including misrepresentations of the law or omissions of fact. Lawyers can buy advertising and use qualified lawyer referral services subject to these regulations.

Often lawyers refer clients to one another, but agreements to do so must not be exclusive. For example, a general practitioner cannot have an exclusive agreement to refer all clients in need of tax help to only one tax attorney. Also, the client must be informed of any referral agreements.

No lawyer may coerce or place a potential client under duress with threats or high-pressure sales tactics. A good example of that is following an airplane crash. Lawyers may not hang around hospitals or visit the homes of survivors or family members to market a prospective client. This would probably be within the rules of decency except that adjustors and lawyers for the airline or their insurance company usually have unfettered access to these same people and often get them to waive their rights for an agreed-to settlement amount.

Any correspondence or electronic communication designed to solicit clients should be marked as an advertisement, unless targeted toward another attorney, family member or someone else who already has a close relationship with the attorney marketing the service.

Many states now allow lawyers to identify themselves as having special expertise in such fields as family law, tax law or criminal law, and the ABA prohibits lawyers from making false claims about these specialties.

Marketing in the Internet Era

When Internet marketing first took hold a mere decade ago, only the most adventuresome attorneys wanted anything to do with it. If you had a "web page," you were marketing something cheap. And no attorney worth his hourly rate would be caught dead in cyberspace.

Then came the emergence of sales sites like E-Bay and payment methods like PayPal, which made E-commerce easier and safer, encouraging people onto the Web to purchase higher-dollar products. Those were the same people who needed higher-dollar legal services (not just cheapie divorces or getting traffic tickets dismissed), so some of the larger law firms began to build their presence on the Web. The first efforts were technically and creatively challenged extensions of firm brochures – a catalog of what the firm does and how the lawyers appear.

Today, although only about one-half of all attorneys in private practice or their firms have Web sites, even the most blue-blood law firms promote 24-hour-a-day advertisements on the Web. One of the first things a savvy consumer of legal services should do is google the kind of attorney you want in the location where you want him.

For instance, try *Family Law Attorney Denver*. At this writing, you bring up 411,000 entries. On the first page of listings, you can browse through the law firms and get the following information:

- General information on divorce, child custody and other family-related matters.
- Facts on the above specifically for Colorado and the Rocky Mountain region.
- Answers to your specific family law questions.
- Media references to divorce and the representations of attorneys listed.
- Invitations to divorce seminars.
- Invitations to subscribe to a family law newsletter.
- Links to information from other sources.
- Links to tell firms about your case.
- Information about the firm's practice areas and individual attorneys.
- Contact information for firms.

For many people wanting to hire an attorney, Web sites have become the first place they look.

It's Best, It's Super, It's Less than Helpful

Changes in the national economy brought about by the Internet have created a new and equally controversial form of marketing – the rise of the comparative ad in lawyer advertising. Since so much print advertising has migrated from newspapers and magazines to the Internet over the past decade, it seems as though every magazine in the country has hit upon a substitute.

Attorneys and other professionals have money and want to be known. Let's honor them and get paid handsomely for it.

So we have the rise of the "Best of" lists, which allow professionals in several fields to stand out in a competitive market for potential clients and lets attorneys distinguish their services from those of others by advertising in rankings touting their status as one of a few "super" or "best" lawyers, recognized for preeminence in a legal market or field of expertise.

Customarily, the publication devises some methodology for allowing them to claim that their selections are the best among lawyers, dentists, doctors, real estate agents and investment advisors. It usually involves some polling of peer groups, plus additional research that results in a list of the preferred people in that field. Those professionals on the list are then offered the "opportunity" to purchase books or ads in special sections of magazines in which the list is published, along with numerous stories about those being honored.

Comparing the quality of one's services with those of other lawyers is often based on vague distinctions among members of the bar and can conflict with an image of the legal community characterized by moderation and decorum. The publications say they prohibit a professional from buying his or her way onto a "best of" list, but let's face it – the goal of these issues is to sell advertising.

No one can convince me that a story about an attorney that talks about his wife and kids and where he likes to have lunch is somehow not influenced by his law firm's regular ads in the "best of" issue. That would be counterintuitive. If you can accept that premise, you must believe that a wealthy businessman will give big money to a political candidate with no expectation of anything in return.

Right over here, I have a bridge to nowhere that I'd like to sell you.

Several states have pushed back against these "best of" lists, requiring disclaimers on every use of the honor. Only the New Jersey bar has steadfastly maintained that such comparisons are false and misleading on their face, since they are virtually impossible to objectively substantiate.

My problem with these lists is not how they affect the legal profession. I think every attorney should turn his or her attention to whether they help or hinder the ability of the public to seek legal services appropriate to their situation.

If an attorney advertises that he is "one of the Best Lawyers in America," does Joe Six-Pack know this means he was listed in a book called *Best Lawyers in America* or does he believe that the lawyer's preeminence in the law is a commonly accepted fact and anyone would be lucky to have the man represent him? If an attorney is selected one of "The Best Lawyers in St. Louis," how many times has the evaluator seen him in court and how many clients has he surveyed? If another attorney fails to be chosen as a "Go-To Lawyer" in his specialty, could it be because he expressed a disdain for local bar activities and is personally not well loved by his peers, although he may be a brilliant courtroom tactician?

Oddly enough, I wonder if the overabundance of "best of" lists has made the attorney search more difficult for consumers. The most comprehensive of these lists is Super Lawyers, compiled by Law and Politics Media.

Every year, Law and Politics Media, with offices in both Minnesota and Washington, selects Super Lawyers (the top 5% of all practicing attorneys) and Rising Stars (top 2.5% of young attorneys) in each state and the District of Columbia. The lists are published along with "advertising opportunities" in the magazine that reaches the greatest number of consumers in the jurisdiction, as well as special Super Lawyer or Rising Stars magazines that go to referring attorneys all across the area.

For instance, the list of Texas Super Lawyers runs in *Texas Monthly*, one of the finest regional magazines in the country. There is plenty of prestige involved in having an ad in this outstanding magazine, and most of the ads or "profiles" are portraits of all the Super Lawyers in the firm sitting on a couch in the firm's lobby or posed against the skyline of their particular city. The first issue that contained Super Lawyers was the largest issue in *Texas Monthly* history. It looked like the Sears catalog. With all of these lawyers and law firms seeking business through the pages of the magazine, that leads us to a question of advertising effectiveness.

I doubt that great numbers of non-lawyers would begin their legal services buying spree by thumbing through page after page of nondescript people in dark suits. There was the occasional short-skirted tough female attorney smoking a cigar or a double-wide plaintiff's lawyer standing in front of his Bentley and cathedral-like house, but most of the photos were deadly dull and said very little about the subject.

The Super Lawyer folks have no definitive information on the effectiveness of their presentation, which is designed to get people through the doors of all these law firms. Super Lawyers has no empirical data about any increases in business for these firms from people reading their profiles. Their sales presentation to advertising attorneys is strictly based on anecdotal information.

Your search to find a professional who can write an acceptable contract, take out a gall bladder, fill a cavity or pick a stock may not be an easy one. All you can do is search out independent opinions, do the research and avoid rushing to a decision.

When You Can't Tell What's Advertising or Journalism

If you think the line between unbiased commentary and advertising has blurred in newspapers and magazines, the line has completely disappeared on radio and television. It's called "pay to play."

In most markets around the country, if professionals—especially doctors, lawyers and those issuing financial advice—want an hour of radio time for their specialty, they can purchase it. No one comes on the air and says this is advertising and the show is produced to sound like a journalistic effort on that topic. The major difference is that the products and services normally sold by the host are promoted on this program. Understand that there is a bias at work and act accordingly. The same holds for many television programs that have "special correspondents" or "service sponsors."

The use of paid placement is growing on early morning programs and programming on syndicated channels. Often the host or another professional interviewer will ask questions of the paying correspondent. If you listen carefully, you can distinguish this interview from one that is strictly journalistic, but they don't announce it. And you need to know the difference.

We have discussed the regulation of attorney advertising. SEC regulations are so restrictive about actual advertising of financial products that you would think they would control the presentation of these programs by those in the investment industry. Without clear, honest information about the performance of a company, funds or other financial instruments, it's tough to invest wisely. Remember that no one should guarantee the future of an investment. With banks, insurance companies, financial advisors and individual brokers all capable of offering investments in various securities, the SEC takes most advertising seriously.

Regulations encourage advertisements that convey balanced information to prospective investors. In particular, rules focus on information regarding an investment's past performance, one gauge of the potential for future success but far from a guaranteed roadmap.

A company must not include a false or misleading statement in information provided to investors. Also, the company should not omit information when doing that would give investors false or misleading understandings of an investment.

Since we know markets fluctuate, it shouldn't be surprising that those who advertise various financial instruments try to trumpet the good times and tap-dance their way around the bad. In 1999 and 2000, when many investment funds grew dramatically, ad campaigns often emphasized favorable short-term gains. Investors received a narrow view of a fund's history. After a market cooling, ads focused on the positive short-term news and not the history or volatility.

In 2003, the SEC amended regulations on advertisements focused on an investment's past performance. An ad lacking an adequate explanation of other pertinent facts might create unrealistic investor expectations or even mislead potential investors. A rule change emphasized a more explicit description of past income, gain, or growth of assets.

At the height of the mortgage and credit crisis of 2008, only the most adventurous companies reeling from the chaos would advertise. Most were satisfied to keep a low profile and wait out the carnage.

The SEC draws specific guidelines for information included in any advertisement for an investment. Exacting rules specify required details and even included wording. An advertisement, for example, must tell an investor to consider the investment objectives, risks, and charges and expenses of the investment company carefully before investing. The ad must explain that the prospectus contains this and other information about the investment company, identifies a source for obtaining a prospectus and states the importance of carefully reading a prospectus.

The rules lay out how and when a prospectus must calculate yields, after-tax returns and other benchmarks. Rules emphasize timeliness of information, requiring the most recent details possible. And regulations even describe presentation, preventing an ad from putting critical details in fine print.

Physician Advertising

Television and print ads tout everything from new drugs that cure impotence to the latest option in plastic surgery. But what about the physician? While a general practice physician, one who might help you fight the flu or make a referral to a specialist, generally does not spend money on pricey advertising, no prohibition prevents the effort.

The American Medical Association issues no restrictions on advertising by physicians, except to protect the public against deceptive practices. A physician may use any commercial publicity such as newspapers, magazines, direct mail, radio or TV to attract patients.

Because the use of medical terms or illustrations can prove difficult to understand, however, physician advertising should break down the information into something digestible by the public. The information must be true and not misleading. The AMA does warn against testimonials of patients who attest to the physician's skill or the quality of the physician's professional services. These ads only reflect one person's results, not the general outcome of patients with comparable conditions. Objective claims, supported by facts about the physician's experience, competence and quality of care, are suitable.

A physician can also include specifics about his or her educational background, details about fees and information regarding the availability of credit or other methods of payment.

Watch out for claims that imply exclusive or unique skills or remedies. Ethics require physicians to share medical advances, making it unlikely that any one doctor offers a truly unique resource. An optometrist might be the only eye doctor in a town with the latest device for laser eye surgery, which he or she could advertise, but it is unlikely the doctor invented the device or uses it in a unique way.

Similarly, the AMA considers it misleading if a physician claims success in treating a large number of cases involving a particular serious ailment in an effort to create unrealistic expectations in prospective patients.

Be Skeptical

No matter the form of advertising or the profession touted, wise consumers take nothing at face value. Rules exist to protect against misleading ads but some television, print and Internet ads push the boundaries in hope of creating an advantage.

Consider an ad a starting point, nothing more. Verify all information before committing time, money or health to anyone. Never shy from skepticism, even if it seems cynical. Skepticism can provide the first line of defense against a misleading ad and a disappointing outcome.

PART THREE

ALL HELL BREAKS LOOSE

15

UPSET, YES, BUT NOT ENOUGH TO SUE

The drama plays out daily, a consistent theme with variations in the actors and scenes. Your lawyer loses a lawsuit that he said was a slam dunk. Your broker recommends an investment that goes sour. Your CPA advises you on a tax shelter and you wind up paying the tax anyway, plus penalties and interest.

The result of this drama is that you feel wronged. The second act begins when you decide to do something about it. And with this step, the plot thickens. You have an understandable passion for revenge and a basic need to win back some, if not all, of your lost money. But you fear that going into the court system might lead to even more losses, frustration and disappointment.

We see this scene unfolding in our practice every day. The vast majority of the cases we handle involve legal malpractice, while the rest involve investment fraud, accounting malpractice and business-to-business fraud. Because malpractice is so difficult to prove and we handle those cases on a contingent fee, we review as many as 100 cases before we settle on one case we feel confident to accept. These statistics are fairly consistent with other firms that specialize in professional malpractice lawsuits. Each of us spend much of our day consoling people and telling them why their cases do not rise to the seriousness of a full-blown lawsuit or are not winnable in the courtroom.

We want people to come away from this experience with the knowledge that they have looked at the situation, consulted with an expert in the field and know they've done their best to cut their losses. Some people want a lawyer to take their case and just send a letter, threatening a lawsuit, but not really intending to go all the way. But that never works. If we take your case and send a letter threatening to sue, we have to mean it.

This was how we saw things after the stock market slide of 2001-2002. I suspect that when the air clears from the current financial crisis, our plate will be full of cases we can win. For many months after a calamity, our conference room is full of investors singing the same sad tune:

Our broker lost us money. Can't we sue?

The truth is that each instance of a broker or wealth manager losing money does not constitute a righteous lawsuit. When your lawyer loses a lawsuit, that is not automatically malpractice. If your CPA confronts the IRS on your behalf but the law says a tax shelter is illegal, you may not be looking at accounting malpractice. Investing involves risk. Lawsuits involve risk. Each case must be examined thoroughly and stand on its own, either as a lawsuit or an upset you will have to come to grips with in another way.

In a few cases with the right facts and circumstances, we say full speed ahead and damn the torpedoes. In the other cases, we tell prospective clients they need to find some other way besides a lawsuit to salve the wounds and get even. This chapter deals with ways your outrage can gain expression short of going to court.

Apologies May Now Be Accepted

Lawyers hate the idea of apologizing for screwing up. They just won't do it and won't let their clients do it in most cases. They feel there's too much liability involved. It has nothing to do with whether or not the client – a hospital, an attorney, an accounting firm or almost any type of professional – is actually guilty of doing harm to someone. They can't figure out how you negotiate your way out of a mess if you go hat in hand, asking forgiveness.

The famous and often-quoted study released in 1999 by the Institute of Medicine estimates that more than one million "preventable adverse events" occur in hospitals each year, resulting in as many as 98,000 deaths from errors that could be prevented. The report set medical organizations to work rooting out those errors. It also set medical personnel on a course of disclosing errors to the public and, you guessed it, apologizing to patients and their families for their foul-ups. Critics of this policy predicted that apologizing would set loose a floodgate of litigation on the medical community, but exactly the opposite happened.

What they found is that most people who are wronged by a doctor's mistake simply want the offending party to say he or she is sorry. In almost 91% of the cases, litigation was either a means to get that apology or a way to punish the wrongdoer for not apologizing.

Programs of disclosure and apology at the Lexington (Kentucky) Veterans Hospital, the University of Michigan Health System, Johns Hopkins, and Children's Hospitals and Clinics in Minneapolis, among others, have resulted in dramatic reductions in legal expenses.

At the Lexington Veterans Administration facility, during a seven-year period, the hospital's average payout was $16,000 per settlement, versus the national VA average of $98,000 per settlement, and only two lawsuits went to trial during a 10-year period. Expenses and the number of lawsuits also dropped in Minnesota, where Children's Hospitals and Clinics of Minnesota reduced the number by half.

Breakdowns in the provider-patient relationship were apparently at the root of nearly 75% of malpractice claims filed against physicians. As odd as this may sound, it is not a fiendish desire to extract money that motivates many victims. It's the fact that their feelings are hurt and the providers don't seem to give a damn.

To counter the perceived risk of increased liability, a number of states have adopted or are considering apology laws that exempt expressions of regret, sympathy, or compassion from being considered as admissions of liability in medical malpractice lawsuits. Federal legislation has also been drafted that promotes medical error reporting, disclosure to patients, apology, and—in cases when the standard of care is not met— offers of compensation.

Filing a Complaint With a State Disciplinary Board

If an apology is not enough for you, or if the provider is reluctant to admit an error, reporting the offending party to a state regulatory board may be in order. Every state has boards or organizations charged with the responsibility of regulating the behavior of attorneys, physicians, dentists, accountants and others.

Some groups take this regulation function seriously, while others act more like trade associations for the professions. But virtually all of the groups have grievance procedures that allow you to file complaints about service errors or omissions.

Some state bar associations aggressively pursue offending attorneys. I will warn you, however, that some states enforce the rules more forcefully on the plaintiff's bar than the defense side or the big firms. Large states split their jurisdictions into districts so that members of their grievance committees will be familiar with other committee members as well as the accused lawyers. In many of these bar groups, committees are not shy about punishing lawyers with suspensions or even disbarment.

The most common offenses are acts of omission – failure to file a lawsuit, show up for a hearing or communicate with a client – plus the mishandling of money.

Medical boards, which receive thousands of complaints about doctors each year, seem to be more lenient on the medical profession than bar groups are on lawyers. A recent story in *The Washington Post* detailed several long histories of doctors with drug problems being given chance after chance to clean up their act.

One doctor was even found to have injected himself with drugs meant for one of his patients during a colonoscopy. The doctor continued the procedure and was seemingly oblivious to the patient's pain. This was only one of a series of offenses, but the doctor was only suspended for a short time and, at this writing, is still in practice.

The process of filing complaints with regulatory bodies can be frustrating, but it is worth the time and effort if committee members listen to and act on your concerns. Even if they do nothing, it may be worthwhile to have your complaint on file, so that the next time someone complains, maybe they will see a pattern and act.

Organization = Evidence = Coherent Story

If you plan to go after the scoundrel who robbed you at pen point, good record keeping is essential. Vital bits of paper, as well as electronic records, can provide crucial evidence for a grievance hearing, settlement of a lawsuit or to help the government put that sorry SOB away for many years.

Managing records, though, can be a nightmare. Kathy Beauchamp, a professional organizer, contracts with individuals and small businesses to help make sense of mounds of information. The most common question asked by her clients? "What do I do with all of my paper?" She offers a few suggestions, as follows:

Decide what to keep

Keep long-term documents you can't replace that are from a reliable source. While a bank might be able to dig out an important check stub, a broker or other business might not maintain a similar archive of information.

The Internal Revenue Service

Always document any information connected to deductions, such as write-offs for education, medical or circumstances such as an adopted child. Keep all of the records with a copy of your tax filing. If the IRS opts for an audit, the protection is essential. As a rule of thumb, maintain these records for at least seven years.

Think Long Term

When a purchase depends on a loan or some other form of long-term credit, be sure to protect the original sales documents. Whether we're talking about a home, yacht, investment or results of a lawsuit — items whose financial responsibility can extend for years — it is easy to misplace documents that spell out the specifics. Keep these documents until the final payment is made and the account is closed.

Organize by Priority

Create an ongoing or pending file. For ongoing projects, such as a home remodel or the purchase of a business, keep all of these documents in one project-specific container. Everything goes in, from a contract to each receipt. At the conclusion of the project, sort through the file and differentiate between items deserving long-term care and those that can go to the shredder. For example, while you might not need to save all research documents connected to a project, finance agreements remain essential.

Secure Storage

For most items, a simple filing cabinet can suffice. Just make sure it's lockable to keep out children or household help. Some documents deserve greater care, such as proprietary business information or transferable stocks. For these items, consider renting a safety deposit box. Imagine a home fire, a disaster by any measure, which can melt the best filing cabinet or even fire retardant safe. For critical documents, a bank, with added security from both theft and fire, just makes sense.

Online Banking

All major banks offer some form of online banking. More than 30% of the nation's households bank online, according to the Online Banking Report, which tracks the industry. For people who must carefully watch their cash flow, such as small business owners, up-to-the-moment updates can become addictive. Also, banks are working to make more information available, such as offering a full year or more of records online.

Banks also recognize the need for security, depending on pentagon-grade systems to guard the data. Users, though, must also take responsibility. Never respond to an email requesting information such as account numbers or a Social Security number. A bank would never seek such details via email. Be suspicious and never hesitate to call a bank and alert them of a possible email phishing scam.

Going Digital

Emphasize paper records, but consider the ever-expanding importance of digital information. A scanner and a desktop database application can turn any computer into a robust data warehouse. Documents become searchable, simple to index and, possibly best of all, they eliminate the need for reams of paper stashed in a filing cabinet.

Going digital, however, brings risks of its own. Foremost is the fallibility of a computer hard drive. Complex devices dependent on platters spinning at wicked speeds, hard drives are destined for failure. Eventually, it happens.

Storage

Because computer hard drives fail, backing up data becomes critical. An external hard drive can provide an affordable option. Typically, these drives link to a computer via a USB cable, and setup is relatively painless. Also, the price of these drives continues to fall, offering more storage space for the dollar.

Most drives include some form of backup software, which automates the copying of critical files from the computer to the external drive. Most modern computer operating systems have similar capabilities built in.

Similarly, it is possible to protect information with dedicated encryption programs. This software puts a password on a digital file, locking it from anyone who doesn't know the proper code. While law enforcement might break the encryption, it should defeat a casual snooper searching through a digital scrap heap.

What happens if a home or business burns, taking that careful backup along with it? Online storage can ease this concern. Read the usage contract to understand the methods the company uses to secure the information. Ask the opinions of tech-savvy friends. Once you decide on the best choice, setting up a system for online storage is relatively simple.

Digital fingerprints do not go away

Assume that every email, online chat, comment on a blog or visit to a Web site leaves a lasting trail. An expert might be required to unearth the specifics, but digital forensics is big business and the number of qualified professionals is growing. Not only does law enforcement hire people capable of searching out the faintest whiff of a digital file to help build cases, but businesses also find these experts essential. Who else could restore a database of critical records if a server crashes?

Too many people believe hitting the delete key or dragging a file into the trash eliminates the information. While some software does promise to eradicate even the faintest bit of information, always assume the worst: Did you write it, file it, email it or post it? Assume someone, somehow can track it down. A subpoena can drag it all into court.

16

A MALPRACTICE LAW SUIT: THE CLIENT'S VIEW

Is there ever enough justice?

My favorite movie about the law is *The Verdict*. In this story of a down-on-his-luck plaintiff's attorney, Paul Newman's character tells his client that the legal system does not guarantee justice. It only gives you a shot at justice.

This is what you get with a legal malpractice lawsuit. Its purpose is not to give you revenge, punish the other side or make sure that rascal never does the same thing to anyone else ever again. Those may be by-products of the lawsuit, but they are not why you are here. In most good cases, the legal system can give you *some* money, and that should make you feel a little better, but the law can seldom give you enough to make you whole again.

The modern legal system is responsible for shaping the most intimate aspects of an individual's life. Who gets the kids after a divorce? Which creditors are paid after a business fails? Who owns the home in a contested will? Many forces orchestrated by an attorney must work in concert to make your effort a success.

The one question that loops through your brain when first meeting with a lawyer to discuss possible legal action is, "Do I have a case?" You should not expect an answer too quickly. In fact, a lawyer too quick to take a case or state the odds of a particular action should make you suspicious.

A lawyer must be willing to spend the time to review the factual record and indicate that he or she will fight for your cause. You want to choose someone capable of making the hard decisions and offering realistic guidance.

No attorney is correct 100% of the time. There's an axiom I recall about law school that demonstrates that fact. It's said that the course you studied hardest for and felt the most confident about is always the one in which you will make your worst grade. And the course you know you failed will produce your best grade.

When weighing the merits of your case, a good attorney intertwines the facts of your case with emotion and his or her passion. When it comes to courtrooms and lawsuits, the lawyer who has the facts on your side, plus the juiciest documents, and presents them with passion usually wins.

Hopefully, you've followed our advice and maintained meticulous records. You want to keep every piece of paper, contract, and correspondence. Note the times and dates of phone calls, and what was discussed. Jot down every pertinent fact, action or conversation in as much detail as possible. Painstaking documentation can tilt the balance of credibility in your favor before a judge or jury.

So, do you have a good case? The most competent attorney should weigh all information, reviewing the complete document record, before offering advice. You should recognize that an initial investment of time can prevent unwise decisions. After all, no one should waste effort, worry and money on a frivolous lawsuit.

A Replacement for Revenge

If your documentation holds up to the initial review and your attorney believes you have a case with merit, make sure you have a "reality check" conversation with the attorney. If a loved one has been lost or horribly injured, the attorney cannot make that person whole again.

In a civil case, we can only help you recover money. A lawyer can never get you enough money to completely make up for your loss. Prepare yourself for a court system that regularly quantifies the dollar value of all forms of human tragedy, such as a child lost during a surgery gone wrong, a man disfigured in a workplace accident, or the disappearance of a retirement nest egg.

Approach a lawsuit and the possibility of a court verdict or settlement as you would a stock tip. If all goes well, an investment of time, effort and money might pay off. Will it make you feel better? Only you can decide.

Evaluating Your Own Case

Once you accept that money rules the legal system, you can make a basic risk assessment, determining the potential financial gain represented by your legal action.

You can take the facts of a case and an attorney's experience and define a realistic financial target on which to base your settlement strategy. For example, if your attorney says your case has a 60% chance of winning a verdict of $1 million, a settlement of $600,000 would be appropriate. The settlement reflects the risk of winning or losing a particular case, with the calculations gaining complexity in proportion to the intricacy of a lawsuit.

Whose decision is it whether you settle or go to trial? Ultimately, that decision rests with you, the client. With your attorney's help, you can decide on a realistic amount that you would take in settlement, a settlement that limits risks but extracts the most from the opposition.

The decision whether to go to trial or accept a settlement is a personal one. There is nothing more satisfying than winning in court. But losing a case in court likely ends the matter. While appeals remain possible in theory, few appeals overturn the loss at trial. The expense of an appeal is often prohibitive. When your attorney approaches you with a proposed settlement, be realistic. Lawyers are often criticized because they want to settle or cannot manufacture a better settlement. The fear that you are being low-balled leads many people to trial. Consider the risk instead. Few people can take that chance, and this reality often shapes settlement offers. I tell clients all the time that if we lose this case, I have another one that I can take to trial waiting for me back at the office. I can make up for my loss. For the client, though, this one lawsuit may be the only chance to get some money back.

When A Winning Verdict is a Loss In Disguise

Big verdicts hit the news often, and one astounding ruling came down in 2000 from a class-action lawsuit in Florida against the tobacco industry. Class-action lawsuits allow many individuals to join together against a defendant. The Florida lawsuit pitted smokers against the cigarette industry and the plaintiffs won $145 billion.

Instead of cashing checks, though, the plaintiffs were tied into a long appeals process. Finally in 2004, an appeals court judge completely threw out the verdict, ruling the case did not deserve class action status since each of the 700,000 plaintiffs had different smoking and medical histories.

The Florida case illustrates an important point: a good settlement usually is better than a great jury verdict, even though some cases will need to be fought out in court. You must accurately assess the strength of your opposition before making that decision. A company with deep pockets may appeal the case to as many courts as possible, finding the expense of appeal far less than paying the award. In other instances, a highly visible company may fear the public relations fallout from a lawsuit enough to pursue a settlement. For both parties, the balance of risk against possible reward determines the outcome.

The moral here is this: settlement is not a dirty word. Wanting to settle is not a sign of weakness. Refusing to consider settlement is often foolish. Each case has to turn on its own facts, and lawyers make mistakes in settlements just like in trial. You do not have to accept any set sum, nor do you have to decide today what you will settle for tomorrow, but be prepared to help your lawyer pursue settlement. If you cannot settle on reasonable terms, get ready to go to court and kick their asses!

17

A Malpractice Lawsuit: How the Lawyer Sees It

No doubt people are upset with lawyers and other professionals for their habits of excess. In the case of lawyers, I've heard people compare us to flesh-eating bacteria and consider this a disservice to the bacteria. Statistics from the American Bar Association show a steady increase in malpractice claims over the past decade, with a majority of the claims against personal injury and family lawyers. These stats are consistent with what we see in our practice. Most of the claims that cross our desk deal with family law. The horror stories people tell make you feel they would have been better represented by the bacteria.

The biggest task for us and other attorneys who handle these cases is to cull out the unwinnable complaints and get down to the cases that can be economically pursued in litigation. Our pursuit, our case review process, is like the story of the little boy who is dropped in a barn, neck deep in horse manure. To everyone's shock, the boy grabs a shovel and starts happily cleaning the stall. When asked about his surprisingly upbeat attitude, the little boy says, "With all of this horse manure, there's got to be a pony in here somewhere."

What a perfect attitude for someone whose job is to screen potential clients for a malpractice firm. The following will tell you what criteria legal malpractice attorneys use to determine which cases to accept.

A World of Conflicts

One of the first things we must determine is whether a new client presents a conflict for the firm. Legal malpractice cases bring up questions you wouldn't consider in any other legal situation. For instance, would we be suing someone we just hired as an expert witness in another case? Could this case affect a personal relationship? (Yes, there are some lawyers with whom we are close personal friends, although because of what we do, that list is short.)

Would this new lawsuit be against a lawyer who is defending one of our other cases and who could, therefore, take out his or her anger on our other client? Conflicts come in every size, shape, color, and stripe and there is no "one size fits all" screening device that can be used. Like the people who work for law firms everywhere, our staff runs the names through our computer system to see if we have had any contact with this lawyer in any context. In the end, though, my partner and I have to look at the name and decide whether we think there is a conflict.

Some lawyers in our area think they are immune to lawsuits by us. They believe we would just not elect to sue them out of professional courtesy. We know this because they express shock when they find out we have taken a case against them. They understand why we would go after "those other guys," but not them. While we remain courteous to everyone in our profession, few attorneys are immune from lawsuits by us or other legal malpractice lawyers. If you are going to put clients first, that means even the lawyers who are professional friends have to come second. Our assistants are trained to secure information in the first telephone interview that is relevant to limitations, venue, and the actual merits of the claim. Within a day or two, the legal assistants meet with the lawyers and present the claims on which there is no conflict and a decision is made by the office on which ones to invite in for a meeting, to further explore their claims. It is important for the prospective client to have a story that my legal assistant can understand. If she doesn't understand it, a jury won't either.

Evaluating the Lawyer's Financial Stake

By the nature of our practice, we take many cases that other lawyers won't touch, but all attorneys have to look at the financial realities of their caseload. A lawyer who sues another lawyer is risking something – standing in the community and the respect of an associate, to name just two things. If you are going to risk the wrath of your fellows, you need to be well paid for your trouble. That's why most people who do legal malpractice work only take cases on a contingent fee basis. I've had prospective clients try to hire me on an hourly basis, believing the other side will fold like a lawn chair when a lawsuit is filed and they will save lots of money. I've also had clients want to pay me hourly only to find later that the case was not such a slam dunk and they would have paid me dearly if I hadn't insisted on the contingency.

In most cases, the fee is calculated based on a percent of the entire recovery, usually from 30 to 45%. Expenses and court costs are usually paid by the client as the case progresses, but sometimes we advance the expenses and then this money is deducted from the client's recovery amount. Our firm policy is that we will not make more on a case than the client, so we never insist on more than 50%, no matter how difficult the case. I just believe that it's immoral for an attorney to profit more than you from your uncomfortable circumstances.

Don't Be the Client Lawyers All Fear

Once conflicts are resolved and questions about payment are answered, we come to the most important element in our decision making about handling a malpractice case – fear of nut jobs! (I rarely use exclamation points, but I feel it is appropriate when discussing the most dangerous client of all!)

At the risk of deeply offending you, the reader, I will tell you about the most fearsome client an attorney can imagine. For whatever reason, legal malpractice cases often attract a rare breed of obsessive character. If someone has been through a case like that, he or she has been through the wringer. It may take an obsessive personality to stay with these cases. But many people we encounter take their anger to an extreme. They get upset when they have to talk to a legal assistant and cannot immediately talk directly to me about their case. Some refuse to write down the facts of the case. I think some people fear these methods will not advocate their cause very well.

In addition, the following are attitudes and actions that would trouble any attorney who handles such cases, and should be avoided by potential clients at all cost:

- Using the word "conspiracy" in almost any context;
- Saying you want to sue the judge;
- Giving the names of five lawyers you have had and what each of the five did wrong;
- Saying you want to sue your opponent's lawyer;
- Claiming your lawyer was bought off by the other side;
- Claiming you have a million dollar case and I can have it all;
- Insisting that a decision has to be made quickly, because

limitations run out in 3 weeks; and

- Quoting case law or statutes to us.

It is helpful to your case to seriously consider these tips about how to approach any legal malpractice lawyer.

What Makes A Case A Winner?

For a legal malpractice case to be winnable and attractive to a malpractice attorney, it needs to contain the following traits and characteristics:

- A clear, concise statement of what the lawyer did wrong. A general complaint that your original lawyer wasn't good and asking me to find out what he did wrong won't cut it.
- An easy-to-understand damage model with significant economic loss that is apparent. Most states do not permit recovery of damages for emotional pain and suffering in a legal malpractice case, so a substantial amount of money must have been lost to justify the expenses of a malpractice case.
- A prompt inquiry that minimizes the chances that we will face a statute of limitations defense because of your delay in hiring counsel. As the old saying goes, "a delay on your part does not constitute an emergency on our part."
- A clever cover-up by the lawyer. Everyone makes mistakes. But the lawyer who tries to cover up his mistakes is the real culprit we like to go after. He or she significantly increases the chance of being sued.

18

THE NUTS AND BOLTS OF A LEGAL MALPRACTICE CASE

Plenty of lawyers out there are filing their first legal malpractice case and basing their entire claim upon the fact that the defendant lawyer violated an ethical rule. An ethical violation is not, however, the same as malpractice. The ethical rules and the comments to the rules help to define the standard of care (as such, violations to the ethical rules are usually admissible in a trial), but they do not establish a right of recovery. A lawyer might, for example, accept representation which, under the ethical rules, should have been turned down because of a conflict, and yet still do a good job for the client. Under that circumstance, the lawyer would have violated an ethical rule but would not have committed malpractice.

Four Major Elements

The four elements of a legal malpractice case are the same as the elements of a car wreck case: duty, breach of the duty, proximate cause and negligence. Prospective clients typically focus on element number two, breach of the duty.

"Let me tell you what my lawyer did wrong."

It is, however, extremely rare that the outcome of a case turns on only whether the lawyer breached the standard of care. Violations of the standard of care have to be proven by expert witnesses, lawyers who are willing to testify against other lawyers.

Of course, even in the most blatant cases, the defendant and his or her insurance company will find a "morally flexible" expert witness somewhere who will testify that the lawyer was not negligent. I had one case where the other side found a lawyer/witness to testify that it was not negligence for the defense attorney in a medical malpractice case to ignore the testimony of the doctor who did the autopsy and prepared the death certificate stating that the woman died of natural causes.

The most significant aspect of proving a breach of the standard of care is typically the cost associated with it: only a lawyer can testify against a lawyer, which means my client and I will have to hire a lawyer as an expert witness and pay that lawyer by the hour to read the file and then testify to the conclusion that everyone already knows—the previous lawyer was negligent. Selection of the right expert witness is one of the most important decisions made in the preparation of a legal malpractice case. I am shocked at the number of lawyers handling these cases who simply use the same lawyer as an expert time after time, without regard to the type of case involved.

A surprising number of cases turn on the issue of duty. The duty inquiry is relatively simple: did the lawyer represent the person now suing her? If so, the lawyer owed that client the duty to act within the standard of care. It is surprising, however, how many lawyers do not know who their clients are. Take that very first legal malpractice case I filed that you read about in Chapter 4: the real estate lawyer was convinced that, although he represented a general partnership of 11 people (in fact, he set up the general partnership), he only owed a duty to the real estate developer who was directing it all. Lawyers who represent business entities are often extremely sloppy about ensuring that they are not representing the individuals who own and manage the business entity. When lawyers discover (by the judge telling them) that they represented more than one client, the rest of the case is usually easy, since lawyers usually only satisfy their obligation of good representation to people they represent.

The Battle Over Proximate Cause

The real battleground in a legal malpractice case, however, usually is proximate cause. In fact, the battleground is usually only one half of the proximate cause element. Law schools take almost a third of your first year of law school to teach these concepts, but I am going to give you a shorter version of it.

Proximate cause consists of two separate inquiries, the "foreseeability" test and the "but for" test. Foreseeability involves the question of whether the damages the client is alleging were foreseeable from the negligent act the client is alleging. For example, in the case I mentioned above, was it foreseeable that the hospital would lose a medical malpractice case if the hospital's lawyer failed to call the doctor who performed the autopsy, to testify that the death was natural? Of course, it is foreseeable, but I have never had a case yet that turned on the foreseeability element in proximate cause.

Ah, the "but for" test. That is the battleground on which I live or die. When I pass the "but for" test, I am off buying new guitars. When I fail, however, I am going through my trash can to find and reuse old guitar strings.

The "but for" test is almost as easy to articulate as the foreseeability test: but for the negligence of the lawyer, would the plaintiff have been spared his claimed damages? Put another way, did the lawyer's negligence cause the damages or were the damages inevitable? I usually illustrate the "but for" test with a medical example. Suppose a terminally ill cancer patient, with only days to live, comes to a doctor and the doctor takes out the patient's appendix. Clear negligence. The patient dies. It was not, however, the doctor's negligence that caused the death. It was the incurable cancer. "But for" the doctor's negligence, the patient would have died anyway.

In that legal malpractice case involving the doctor who was not called to testify, I asked the client, our expert and myself: "What would have happened if the lawyer had called the doctor who did the autopsy?" To win on this point, I have to demonstrate at trial that changing the lawyer's negligent act to a non-negligent act (calling the doctor instead of not calling the doctor), results in a different and better outcome for the client.

When a legal malpractice claim is based on previous litigation, the "but for" test is described as the "case within a case." To win such a legal malpractice case, I must not only prevail on the four elements of the legal malpractice negligence claim, but also I must retry and prevail on the underlying case: the case within a case. How to win that issue is the magic to handling legal malpractice cases for the plaintiff.

Both Sides Want to Control Litigation

There are plenty of roadblocks to success in the legal malpractice area. In most cases, it's like fighting two lawsuits at once – the original case that burned you and this new one against the lawyer who did the burning.

Litigators in this practice area like to believe they will go to the mat for their clients in the courtroom every day. Professionals, the firms they work for and the insurance companies that wind up paying the bill want to feel they will fight when necessary, too. But the uncertainty of litigation has fueled a move toward alternate forms of dispute resolution, which I explain in the next two chapters.

19

THE MANY FORMS OF ALTERNATIVE DISPUTE RESOLUTION

Our nation's founders meant for the courts to protect every citizen, but a new series of locks now appear on the doors to our legal system. Sometimes, you must unlock them before or instead of making it to court.

The concept is called alternative dispute resolution (ADR). It originates out of the belief that there is too much litigation, that courtrooms are crammed with litigants, shoulder to shoulder, seeking relief. ADR provides a way to settle disputes without the expense or hassle of court. But in at least some of the cases, it also operates without many of the safeguards that having your day in court was intended to provide.

Did you know that most modern contracts include clauses prohibiting you from ever filing a civil lawsuit. You've probably already signed contracts relinquishing or limiting your legal rights and you never even realized your loss, and won't until you need the protection of the courthouse.

Just about every contract, whether with a car dealer, a homebuilder or software manufacturer, includes a clause demanding some form of

ADR. These agreements control how your dispute will be handled outside the court system, including where the case is heard and who pays for what. In many cases, ADR is the only option.

Consider a family who buys a new house from a homebuilder, only to find that workers used inferior wood to frame the home. A few months after moving in, warped walls and sagging doorways make the house unliveable. Months of complaints follow, with the family finally calling a lawyer who points to an ADR clause in their contract.

The agreement demands arbitration and mandates that any hearings occur in the homebuilder's home state, 1,000 miles from the family's house. The family must arbitrate the dispute, with a third party chosen from a list provided by the homebuilder as the decision maker. And the family has no right to appeal the decision.

The unfairness of this is palpable, but what is your recourse? Our courts, all the way up to the U.S. Supreme Court, have ruled these agreements enforceable, even preferred. The family willingly entered into the contract to buy the home. By doing so they accepted every aspect of the contract and its ramifications.

ADR consists of several recognized methods, depending on the type of case and the contractual situation. Those methods are traditional negotiation, mediation, collaborative law and arbitration. They are listed here along a continuum from voluntary to binding. In this chapter, we will discuss the forms of ADR that are non-binding.

Informal, Around the Table

Sometimes called a settlement conference or the kitchen table approach, traditional negotiation is the oldest and most common method of resolving conflicts without actually going to court. The mechanics of this are simple: two attorneys agree to meet in a conference room, on the golf course or over a beer and hash out the details of settlement. Sometimes the warring parties are present, at other times it's just the lawyers armed with whatever discovery documents they have obtained, plus their wits.

Traditional negotiation is completely fair to both parties because you are on equal footing. You do not have to meet, but if you do and reach a settlement, you agree to accept any terms of settlement reached in the session.

Mediation

Mediation creates a viable and increasingly commonplace alternative to going to trial, allowing you to avoid the expenses and risks of court. The litigants and their counsel work with a neutral third party who attempts to negotiate an agreement. The theory is, the lawyers cannot do it alone.

Mediation can prove valuable in situations where the courts are ill equipped to reach a judgment, such as in family law. Rather than asking the court to decide who gets to keep the family home or which divorcing parent should have the children, mediation allows parents to work out a plan acceptable to everyone. Also, mediation can often conclude a divorce more quickly and with less expense and less conflict than litigation.

This method actually got its start in family law, and it's been in wide use in the domestic relations courts for about 25 years. The only thing binding about mediation is that many family court judges require the parties to go through the mediation process before he will hear their case in court. Participation is mandatory, but the system itself is nonbinding, meaning you can walk away and refuse to settle if you want your day in court.

Lately, this principle has extended to other types of civil disputes. When an investment counselor steals from you or when a business partner runs off with the profit, civil courts may order mediation. In many instances, the only way you are going to get any money back is with the help of a good referee and doses of old fashioned common sense and compromise.

"Nothing bad can happen to you in mediation, because nothing will happen unless in the end you reach an agreement," says Will Pryor, a mediator who has worked in nearly 2,000 cases.

Consumers should pay close attention to mediation, because more and more businesses include a mediation clause in their contracts. These clauses require mediation before you are allowed to file a lawsuit, instead of after.

Two or three decades ago, industries such as insurance and banking accepted that daily business would generate a number of customer lawsuits. "Litigation was just another line item in their budget," Pryor says. These institutions, however, eventually recognized that mediation could save money, prevent or shorten lawsuits and keep disputes private and confidential. "A notion took hold that businesses might as well use mediation before a suit because the court would make them mediate anyway," Pryor says.

While popular with businesses, mediation can also benefit consumers. "In many respects, it's a consumer-friendly opportunity," Pryor says. "It levels the playing field and gives the consumer, in theory, a chance to meet a decision maker on the other side."

Business partners arguing over a transaction, neighbors in a tussle over an oral contract or two family members fighting over a relative's will could all opt for mediation before going to court. No preexisting contract is necessary, and triggering mediation requires nothing more than a decision by all parties involved.

A decade ago, 90% of mediations took place *after* lawsuits were filed. Now, about 50% choose that process *before* filing.

How Mediation Works

Participants in each case can shape the specifics of the mediation by agreement. Location is usually left to the mediator, and it is usually a neutral site. Though one party might try to intimidate the other, most attorneys and mediators appreciate that this violates the spirit of mediation. More importantly, overtly trying to rig the process almost guarantees failure. Remember, no one has to accept an agreement, and creating an antagonistic atmosphere from the get-go does no one any good. Lawyers have to learn to present your case fairly and passionately. And they have to present it without causing unnecessary offense, although some offense is natural when you have to hear what you find disagreeable.

Here are some key features of mediation that you, as one of the parties, will want to be aware of and approve. The key player in this form of dispute resolution is the mediator, a neutral party with whom you will want to feel comfortable. The mediator might be an attorney specializing in ADR, a retired judge, an expert in the particular topic being mediated or a non-lawyer specifically trained in mediation.

You and the other side can present lists of potential mediators and negotiate the final selection. Then the mediator works with the two parties to set a date and time for the meeting. Usually, mediation occurs at the mediator's office. Mediation is typically scheduled for half-day or full-day sessions, depending on the complexity and level of animosity. In most cases, a second session is not scheduled. Although you can agree to meet again, it may be more productive to consider that this session must resolve matters for the mediation to succeed.

The mediator usually opens with a five- or 10-minute explanation of the process intended to settle everyone's nerves. "I usually tell people we're not here to win or lose, but to have a conversation and through that we can understand each other's perspective and hopefully come to an agreement." Pryor says. The mediator's opening remarks define the issues at stake and areas of agreement and disagreement.

After these introductory remarks, each side presents their side of the dispute, to help the mediator understand and show the other side the risks of going to court if the disagreement is not settled.

Few mediations proceed with the parties face-to-face. Instead, the mediator shuttles between two conference rooms, listening to proposals and searching for common ground between the parties. Each party can confide confidential information to the mediator, who must keep that information private.

The mediator looks beyond the offers, seeking areas of common interest to find a middle ground on which to build consensus. "What you're doing is constantly looking beneath the surface to understand the position each party is taking," Pryor says.

Someone once said that a settlement succeeds when both sides are dissatisfied. "The process makes it likely that you'll get some satisfaction, but it almost eliminates the possibility that you are totally satisfied," Pryor explains.

For example, a homeowner hops on his brand new riding lawnmower. The brakes fail, the mower plows into a play structure and the homeowner's young son is knocked to the ground, causing a head injury that requires hospitalization. The homeowner and manufacturer agree to mediation before going to court. The customer believes he should be reimbursed for the child's medical expenses, plus money for pain and suffering, damage to the play set and a new mower. The manufacturer contends the problem was entirely operator error and offers nothing.

The mediation results in an agreement for medical expenses and a new mower with better brakes. The manufacturer does not agree to pay for pain and suffering and the homeowner will fix the minor damage to the play set. Compromise. Middle ground.

Pryor says that if both parties can reach agreement, he prepares documents outlining the specifics. Often other documents, such as confidentiality agreements, are required but those prepared at mediation can end the core dispute. Once an agreement appears on the table, everyone must make a decision. Either side can walk away, moving the case along to court. Once both parties sign the agreement, however, the document becomes binding and each side must follow through with any actions defined by that agreement.

Deciding When to Accept a Mediated Agreement

Whether you decide that hiring an attorney to mediate your settlement makes sense may depend on the amount at issue and the facts of the case.

Consider a family at odds with an insurance company over the company's refusal to pay for a $10,000 surgery for the family's child. The insurance contract requires mediation before any lawsuit, and the family goes through the process in good faith but wants the insurer to pay for the full cost of the operation.

In the final agreement, the insurer offers to pay $5,000 and the family must weigh that offer against the risk of going to court and possibly getting the entire $10,000, interest and attorney fees. An attorney could help define the odds of winning in court. For example, the lawyer might determine this case only has a 20% chance of winning at trial, with a loss leaving the family with nothing. Given those odds, the mediated agreement might look good to the family.

Some Investment Necessary

Whether or not you hire an attorney, you will have some investment in the process. The parties usually split the cost of the mediator, which can run to several thousand dollars for a full-day session.

"Whether it's a small matter or something that will settle for millions of dollars, the fact people have committed their time and pushed a check across the table to the mediator invests them in the process," Pryor says. "All of us want to get something for our money."

While still an organized process with a clear framework, mediation is the most flexible form of ADR. For instance, most mediations work best with each party separated from the other. But sometimes bringing two parties together face-to-face can clear up a surprising number of disputes. If a daylong mediation fails to get results, Pryor sometimes asks the principals involved to meet one-on-one, without lawyers present.

Consider a two-year-old falling out between business partners and long-time friends. One grew angry over how the other spent company money and hired a lawyer, forcing the other partner to up the stakes by also hiring a lawyer. The case boiled for months and was headed for court before one of the attorneys suggested mediation.

Pryor says that if he believes the anger has ebbed, he asks the two former friends to meet alone and see if time, perspective and the threat of a courtroom battle can help settle the disagreement. "Their response, almost 100% of the time, is 'We can do that'?" With mediation, the goals extend beyond the process. Creating a resolution and avoiding court matters most.

Collaborative Law: Can We All Just Get Along?

The newest and most interesting form of ADR is called collaborative law. It was developed in the 1990s, again by family lawyers who wanted to find a better way to resolve family law disputes without the destruction and expense often resulting from litigation. They developed collaborative law as a sort of super mediation process that operates entirely outside the traditional court adversary system. The two cornerstones of the collaborative process are the duty of full disclosure of information and the requirement that the collaborating lawyers withdraw if the dispute cannot be resolved by settlement. If there is a matter pending and the parties decide to try collaborative law, they sign a formal participation agreement and inform the court.

Unlike mediation where the parties are in separate rooms, the collaborative process brings the parties and their attorneys together in the same room, usually in the office of one of the attorneys. Rather than one marathon session, meetings are normally two hours in length and follow an agenda created jointly by the attorneys. The attorneys also work together to tamp down disagreements and keep the sessions moving. Cases can settle in as few as three or four meetings, although the more complicated cases take longer.

"The process is driven by interest-based negotiation more than traditional positional bargaining," says family lawyer Kevin Fuller. "It works better because people attack the problem instead of each other. By focusing on the shared and competing interests and concerns of each party, a win-win resolution can be more easily discovered than by focusing on what a court or jury will do with a certain set of facts."

Critics of this method maintain that only people who get along in the first place can possibly reach agreement under these circumstances. Fuller maintains that just like in mediation, conflict in collaborative law is managed rather than absent. Family law cases comprise most of the legal matters employing collaborative law, but lawyers are beginning to use this process in a wide variety of civil actions where participants don't want to engender the anger and recriminations present in litigation.

For instance, in business disputes where both the business and its supplier want to maintain a working relationship even though there is a dispute, collaborative law could be used to resolve the dispute without destroying the relationship between the business and its supplier.

Probably the greatest pushback against collaborative law comes from lawyers who have little faith in a method where they are forced to cooperate with the other side. A unique feature of collaborative law is that if the attorneys can't settle the case and it goes back into the court system, the collaborating attorneys must withdraw and be replaced by new attorneys. Many attorneys dislike this feature because it keeps them from making the money from taking the case to court.

Collaborative law started in the Midwest and migrated to California, where it has been exported to the world. Attorneys in many parts of this country are beginning to use this process, which is widely practiced in Canada, Great Britain and Western Europe.

Should You Settle?
Yes, If the Offer Is Right

We say you should settle your lawsuit if the offer is reasonable, and now a study shows that's the smart way to go.

A recent study published in the *Journal of Empirical Legal Studies* found that most plaintiffs who pass up a settlement offer and go to trial get an average of $43,000 less than if they had taken the offer.

The vast majority of cases settle, from 80% to 92% by some estimates. The researchers looked at the amount plaintiffs were offered in settlement and compared those to the amounts people actually received after a trial. The findings suggest that some lawyers may not be explaining the odds to their clients, or clients are not listening to their lawyers.

As part of the study, the biggest of its kind to date, the authors surveyed trial outcomes over 40 years until 2004. They found that poor decisions to go to trial have actually become more frequent. This study took into account the lawyer's experience, rank of a lawyer's law school and the size of his or her law firm. More significant was the type of case and the fee arrangements.

Plaintiffs were wrong about proceeding to trial in 61% of the cases, as opposed to 24% of those on the defense side that were wrong. But while more plaintiffs made the wrong decision, the consequences were worse for defendants.

When a defendant in a lawsuit failed to settle, it cost an average of $1.1 million more after going to trial.

20

ARBITRATION: ADR OF THE BINDING KIND

They are hiding in plain sight, all those codicils and addenda to contracts. They are presented as a way to simplify disputes. But they are the ones you have to overcome in your pursuit of those who did you wrong. Practically every contract you sign these days has an arbitration clause, and that *always* benefits big business over the individual. Arbitration rulings are binding, leaving you with no option to appeal. Get a set of arbitrators who don't buy your view of things and your route to recovery is completely blocked.

Once, the court frowned on arbitration, refusing to enforce such clauses. Contracts containing arbitration clauses had to spell out the specifics in big red letters, making sure no one would miss the details. Now, arbitration clauses might appear only in the fine print of a contract, and in places most people would not look. Have you ever purchased software and ignored the block of legalese that appears as you install it? Next time, read it all. You will probably find an arbitration clause buried inside.

The clause will often establish that the case will be heard far from your home, specify that the laws of another state will apply, set absurb payment guidelines and generally put the business in an advantageous position. In the case of stockbroker and other investment fraud, arbitration has evolved into the protector of those who would cheat you in the name of free enterprise.

With courts supporting these contracts containing clauses limiting your ability to go to court, you must take responsibility for what you sign. Read each contract closely. If you do not like the options, buy from someone else or try to negotiate a change, such as demanding non-binding mediation over binding arbitration. My son routinely marks out the arbitration clauses in every contract he signs, and so far no one has called him on it. Many businesses, though, are so anti-consumer that they would rather lose a customer than expose the company to the possibility of facing you in court.

In the late 1990s, Gateway computer created one of the biggest stirs, says mediator and arbitrator Will Pryor, with several cases expanding the reach of such clauses and making arbitration even more unfair to their customers. In the carton of each computer sold, the company included a piece of paper explaining that any dispute must go to arbitration for settlement. Accepting the computer implied the customer's consent, even if the customer never read the document crammed in with all of the other instructions, warranties and solicitations. Many of the terms were not even included with the products and could be ascertained only by contacting a company office in France.

Gateway included a provision that arbitration must occur at the home office of the company, forcing an upset consumer to travel to the company rather than to a neutral site. And some customers even had to pay Gateway for the privilege of getting arbitration. In the main case of several involving Gateway, use of the arbitration clauses was upheld.

Investment Fraud Arbitration

In the period after the 2002 stock market slowdown that I wrote about before, many of the people who crowded into our conference room were there because a stockbroker or wealth manager lost money for them. As happens in every down period, everyone was losing money. It seemed they were all in our conference room demanding retribution from their brokers.

Claims against stockbrokers rarely go to trial but are instead decided by a panel of arbitrators. One of the three arbitrators has to be a member of the industry, a fellow stockbroker. And we found during that time that if you are among the first people in a cycle to take part in arbitration, you have a much better opportunity to recover at least some portion of your investment.

As time went along, though, we saw arbitrators begin to stiffen in their opposition to these plaintiffs. Arbitrators heard essentially the same story from thousands of damaged people, and they began to tire of it. We saw that after the first few wins for our side, the brokers and their companies began to get the best of it, even with clients we knew were telling the truth. Even brokers who admitted to falsifying documents were winning. Like with many things in life, timing is as important as a just cause. If you think you have a case against a stockbroker or other investment counselor, don't hesitate. File your claim as quickly as possible to be at the head of the line in a down cycle.

Even before the financial meltdown of 2008, we were in the midst of an erratic growth period, when stocks would drop dramatically for a few days, then go back up for several more. In this period of stagnant or deflating stock portfolios, attorneys are representing a growing number of investors seeking damages against a stockbroker for the following types of improper action:

Unsuitability

Federal regulations require brokers to suggest only investments that are appropriate or well suited to their clients' individual needs and circumstances.

Churning

Brokers whose compensation is based partly on the number of shares traded must not suggest trades simply to pad their own accounts.

Unauthorized Trading

Brokers are required to gain authorization for trades from their clients and not purchase stocks for a client without authorization.

Fraud

These are the very lies and misrepresentations that have made people suspicious of stockbrokers and money managers for decades.

If your situation involves an element of one of these actions, and you can prove it, you have a shot at recovery in arbitration.

A Framework for Arbitration

The American Arbitration Association (AAA) is a not-for-profit organization committed to the use of arbitration, mediation and other ADR procedures to end disputes. While no law requires anyone to follow the association's guidelines, they help us understand the basic steps involved. In 2006, more than 137,000 cases were filed with the organization. Areas of dispute included commercial law, construction, labor and insurance. Each arbitration agreement takes its own form, but the association provides guidelines for how it approaches arbitration of a range of issues. When someone goes to the association for help, the AAA processes a case from filing to closing, including the appointment of arbitrators, setting the hearings and transmitting documents.

Arbitrators are independent third parties and are not employees of the association. In a consumer case, the arbitrator may be a lawyer, unless the parties agree otherwise. In a case with many financial details, for example, the parties might choose an accountant to decide the matter.

Before hearing a case, the arbitrator must guarantee neutrality, completing a checklist to identify any past or present relationship with either party, witnesses or either party's lawyer or representative. Any connections between the arbitrator and anyone else involved are disclosed to both parties, who can then decide whether or not the arbitrator should remain.

The AAA has rules specific to consumers involved with business contracts containing standardized arbitration clauses. One point to consider is cost. If a consumer's damage claim does not exceed $10,000, the consumer's cost is $125. If the claim is $10,001 to $75,000, the consumer's cost is $375. The business must assume all other costs.

A consumer unable to pay the fees can apply for a waiver, allowing a hearing to go forward at no cost to the individual. In many instances, an arbitrator can rule on a case after a review of documents. Either party to a dispute, however, can demand a hearing.

A Strategic Outline

The process begins when someone demands arbitration. A consumer can challenge a company, or in some cases a business may challenge a consumer. Regardless, this action starts the proceedings, allowing 15 days for the other side to respond or issue a counterclaim.

The next step focuses on selection of an arbitrator, allowing input from both parties as to the qualifications required by AAA. Each side receives a list of possible arbitrators, including biographies. The association encourages agreement but will appoint someone if necessary.

A preliminary hearing, usually via conference call, is the first discussion of the case with the arbitrator, who helps to identify the steps required before an evidentiary hearing. This meeting also establishes a schedule for the exchange of information, such as witness lists and, in complex cases, pre-hearing briefs. Both parties then have time to complete this work and exchange information in preparation for a hearing.

Some hearings are decided in face-to-face meetings. Others occur via conference call. Still others might hinge on a simple review of pertinent documents. Typically, a small arbitration case can be completed in less than five months from start to finish, while large cases can take years.

Usually, the party filing the arbitration presents evidence first, and formal rules of evidence common in courtrooms do not apply. While the standard may differ in the more casual setting, a consumer must come prepared with sufficient evidence to prove his or her side of a dispute. Simply stating the details of a perceived slight will not work. Documents and testimony provide the backbone of any successful action.

After the hearing, the arbitrator might allow a time for additional submissions, such as providing documentation unavailable at the hearing.

Finally, the arbitrator will determine any applicable award, normally within 30 days after closing the record. In some states, the arbitrated agreement must be "confirmed" in a court of law. The consumer has almost no opportunity to appeal this ruling.

Whether buying consumer electronics equipment, ordering goods by mail or entering an agreement for an exterminator to treat a home, you may come in contact with this process. You might consider the loss of the right to sue reasonable in many cases. After all, the cost of going to court might quickly exceed the cost of the goods or services. Just make sure you recognize the risk. The choice is yours.

21

IF YOU GO TO COURT

When faced with a contentious dispute, whether with a business partner, corporation or even a family member, you can threaten to challenge them in court. A victim might hope for a serving of revenge, a way to recoup money lost in a bogus transaction or possibly an end to a bad business relationship. What he is sure to get, if his case goes to trial, is a completely new experience.

A trial is always a possibility for anyone who either initiates or is the target of a lawsuit. Don't file without understanding the risk in time and money. You will want to know your way around the courthouse.

Understanding the Court System

According to the America Bar Association, state courts handle more than 95% of cases. Divorce, traffic violations and most criminal matters that don't involve crossing state lines all play out in state courts.

Trial courts are where initial rulings are made. Sometimes it is possible to seek additional relief in an appeals court, but an appeal is much misunderstood. It is not a "do-over.' Appeals courts focus on mistakes or misinterpretations made by a judge in the initial trial, not a rehearing of the case. Don't expect to try the entire proceeding over.

Each state has a high court that can issue a final ruling on state law. The U.S. Supreme Court is the final stop. The Supreme Court hears relatively few cases that deal with broad legal concepts, so your case has to have some "higher meaning" to even be heard.

When contemplating legal action, venue is all important. Venue means what court will hear a case, and in many instances venue can sway an outcome. Just as no two people are exactly the same, no two judges or juries in different counties will necessarily render the same judgment, even when presented with identical facts. As a result, each court has its own tenor, often resulting in divergent results. One court might prove friendlier to business. Another may swing toward the plaintiff. The shifts depend on the judges and their specific legal philosophies and the people who serve on juries.

Consider a financial services company with a home office in Atlanta and satellite offices in Birmingham, Houston and Oklahoma City. Five brokers in the Oklahoma office conspire to improperly pump up the value of a stock, ultimately costing investors thousands of dollars. A criminal case convicts the brokers and an investor-driven civil suit goes after the company for damages. If the investors' attorneys perceive a more client-friendly court in Georgia, they argue that the case belongs in the company's home city of Atlanta. Meanwhile, the company's lawyers might argue to keep the case in Oklahoma, home to the regional office, if they find through research that Oklahoma is more pro-defense.

Courts in each state honor local laws, with no two states operating the same. Some states elect their supreme court judges. In others, the governor appoints the justices. Similarly, laws and the inner workings of each court system differ, often dramatically. Don't hesitate to ask an attorney to explain the specifics for your jurisdiction.

The Pretrial Windup: Discovery

No matter the court or venue, the justice system tries to level the playing field between the accused and accuser. For someone taking on a big company or a wealthy individual with extensive resources, a process called discovery can provide needed specifics, or it can be your undoing.

Discovery allows the gathering and disclosure of information before mediation or trial. This process should allow equal and fair negotiations during settlement talks and, if a case goes to trial, limit ambush-style surprises.

Discovery can require everyone involved not only to produce documents and records but also to respond to questions from the other side both orally and in writing. Trials and mediation rely on discovery, and they couldn't function without it. The process can unearth a wealth of information.

Following are the main elements of discovery in any court case:

Interrogatories — These are written questions, which must be answered truthfully. Interrogatories, usually issued early in the process, can catch someone off-guard if they are unaware of an answer's consequences. Often answers to these questions provide a foundation for the case. You may have to answer these questions yourself. Discuss the interrogatories with your attorney to determine the best response.

Request for Production of Documents — An attorney can demand specific documents needed to prepare a case. For a business, these requests can prove damaging and a company's lawyers may seek hearings to attempt to keep many records out of the trial process. These requests can unlock a complex case. A refusal to produce a harmful document can result in severe sanctions for the offending party.

Request for Admissions — With written questions, attorneys can ask either party to admit or deny specific facts. An attorney may ask the opposing party to agree to some basic facts in a case. In an instance of two business partners contesting an issue, each might agree to the business' basic financial structure and other non-contested points so they don't have to waste the court's time establishing those facts.

Depositions — Often the most confrontational and important tools of discovery, depositions are taken in person, under oath. A deposition can uncover the basis for the opposition's case as well as the substance of witness testimony. Any allowable question must be answered and your attorney will be present to protect you against unfair questions. Revealing too much too easily can help your adversary, while being evasive can earn you a sanction from the court. Depositions are formal legal proceedings, not conversations. While you must answer truthfully and completely, your attorney should prepare you to answer correctly. A court reporter will note everything said during a deposition to create a written record. Each party to the case may use the transcript at trial.

The Motion Practice

The time before your case actually goes to court is taken up with a variety of motions. If you are the plaintiff, the defense will almost assuredly make a motion to the court to dismiss the case. If the motion is granted, you are out of the courthouse and back on the street. If the motion is denied, other motions will be made that shape the case, such as those involving any evidence that attorneys hope to include or exclude from the case.

A case is often reset more than once before actually reaching trial. Continuances, the postponement of a trial, occur for a variety of reasons: the parties may not be ready to try the case, the attorneys or their clients may have conflicting schedules or the court might have a full docket that week. A case may receive a continuance if the judge is already in trial on another case, has an immediate issue to address or has an older case to hear.

These delays are not unusual, but you can't count on them. Remember the case involving plaintiff Howard Byrnes and his attorney, Charles Bundren. The attorney took it for granted that he could get a continuance in the case. When he didn't get it, the case blew up around him.

Appearing in Court

On the morning you're going to court, whether for a hearing or the actual trial, take the experience seriously. Dress with respect for the system. If you're not sure about your wardrobe choices, consult your attorney. Image is important when speaking to a judge or jury. In a dispute involving finances, your credibility is on the line from the start. It's subtle, but you want to appear worthy of a successful outcome.

Remember to set a place to meet your attorney at the courthouse. Judges are assigned their own courtrooms and the most likely places to meet are in nearby hallways. To reach most courtrooms, you must usually pass through a metal detector. Do not carry anything possibly considered a weapon or anything that might set off the alarm, including mace canisters or large key chains.

When you appear in court, always act in a mature and professional manner. Emotion-fueled threats, even violence, have marred court actions. Judges see this type of behavior and clamp down with a zero tolerance policy.

Always approach your day in court with a calm, cool exterior, even if a swarm of butterflies is turning flips in your stomach. Some cases settle because one party appears so confident in court that he or she scares the other side. As in most things in life, the individual who keeps the emotions in check usually wins.

Courtroom Cast of Characters

Here are the titles and functions of some people you will encounter in the courtroom:

Judge — The judge conducts the proceedings. He or she is responsible for ensuring that both sides of a case follow the rules established by law and any pre-trial decisions. The judge carries the burden of being unbiased, viewing both sides unemotionally. In some cases, a judge may also give a final ruling in a case that determines the outcome or issue a judgment that determines a financial award.

Bailiff — This is a uniformed officer of the court who keeps order and enforces the wishes of the judge. If one party gets belligerent and the judge holds him or her in contempt, the bailiff takes that person to jail.

Court Clerk — This person manages the court, including handling all the paperwork necessary for a hearing or trial, posting the court's docket and dealing with the demands of litigants and attorneys. Usually, the clerk is not in the courtroom during proceedings, but you may have dealings with him or her.

Court Reporter — This person's job is changing with advances in technology. Court reporters traditionally take down everything said in court and prepare transcripts for later trials and appeals.

Jury – Usually consisting of 12 people, a jury listens to the facts of the case. Once lawyers wrap up their arguments, a judge typically reads the specifics of the law the jurors must then consider. The jury interprets these instructions and applies them to the testimony heard in the case to reach a judgment.

Law Clerks – These are recent law school graduates who may be doing research for the judge and will be seen coming in and out of the court during proceedings.

Keep Composed on the Stand

The image presented from the witness box is critical. Focus on the issue at hand. Sit up straight. Speak clearly and be polite. Remember the judge or jury evaluates your responses and your overall demeanor. While on the witness stand, do not argue with the other lawyer or answer questions in a haughty or sarcastic fashion.

Be wary of the opposing counsel. Do not try to be clever. If you feel you're facing an attack, do not strike back. The other side may try to get you upset and alter your focus. Do not help them achieve their goal. You are not trying to win an argument with the other attorney. Your target is the judge or jury, and that is a very different goal.

When the other side questions you, give truthful and accurate answers. Lying on the stand is unethical, illegal and impractical. All it takes to ruin your credibility with the trial judge or jury is to be caught lying on the stand one time, even about some insignificant fact.

Offering more information than the other lawyer requests can prove the other side's case. Once you answer the question as briefly as possible, don't say another word. If you are concerned about how to answer certain questions, discuss this with your lawyer.

Your lawyer should detail a specific plan for handling the case at trial, based on the information available. (You may think a fact or piece of evidence is absolutely essential, but it could be unnecessary to the judge and throw your lawyer off stride.) Most lawyers want to know how you will testify. Taking your lawyer's advice is essential to your case. Everyone worries about not remembering dates. Don't worry. We all have trouble remembering dates. Do not, however, take any notes with you to the stand without clearing it with your lawyer.

Basic Rules for Giving Testimony

- Always tell the truth.
- Always tell the truth.
- Always tell the truth.
- Listen to the question.
- Make certain you understand the question before answering.
- Be sure to answer the question, don't avoid it.
- Take your time.
- Answer only the question asked.
- Answer orally and distinctly.
- Do not guess.
- Avoid boxing yourself in.
- Don't argue with the opposing counsel.
- If you forget the question, ask the attorney to repeat it.
- Dress appropriately.
- It is okay for witnesses or your attorney to have spoken to you.
- Do not respond to the question until the opposing attorney completes the question.

Legal Cannibalism: A Promising Trend For Those Injured By Attorneys

There was a time when lawyers wouldn't go after their own kind. That time is no more, and this is good news for clients who wish to level the playing field for themselves and other laypersons.

In 2007, a clash of legal titans occurred, with king of torts Joe Jamail suing his fellow Houston trial lawyer, John O'Quinn, for $35.7 million in expenses and penalties from breast implant litigation.

The suit stemmed from a 1999 action claiming O'Quinn unlawfully took funds from the settlements due more than 3,000 clients. One of the lawyers estimated that with interest and attorney fees, O'Quinn could pay up to $60 million out of his estimated $263.4 million in fees from breast implant cases. That's certainly not enough to impoverish the hugely successful O'Quinn, but a verdict in favor of Jamail's clients would take a big chunk out of trial lawyer pride.

What makes this case so important is that Jamail, who won the largest jury verdict in history in *Texaco v. Pennzoil*, did not hesitate to take on another player in the high stakes litigation game.

O'Quinn has recorded some of the largest jury verdicts in history, also, and was one of the lawyers the state of Texas hired to win a large settlement from the tobacco companies back in the 1990s.

What this shows is that no one is above the law and rules of common sense. When a lot of money changes hands, there's a group of lawyers chasing it. Whoever makes the money will get sued, whether it's a doctor, car manufacturer or lawyer. It used to be that if a lawyer like John O'Quinn treated his clients incorrectly, few attorneys of any stature would get involved.

We are now entering the era of what I call legal cannibalism, when top litigators will go after their own. You can see dollar signs everywhere that people like O'Quinn and Jamail practice their craft. But when lawyers sue lawyers, something beyond money comes into play, especially when two nationally renowned lawyers go after each other.

The practice of trial law involves a lot of ego. When O'Quinn goes up against Jamail, I promise you, it isn't only about the money. At this writing, a court has ruled in favor of Jamail. Whatever the outcome, the result is a fairer litigation climate for the average person.

22

WHAT THEY DID
WAS CRIMINAL

When two name partners of the best-known shareholder law firm in the country go to jail for their excesses, something has been lost in our struggle to protect ourselves from being robbed at pen point.

William Lerach and Melvyn Weiss of Milberg Weiss Bershad Hynes & Lerach were the kings of shareholder suits against many of the major corporations in the nation. They recently pled guilty to a kickback scheme that provided secret payments to lead plaintiffs in securities class-action suits brought by Milberg. The payments rewarded the lead plaintiffs with more money than they would have gotten as members of the class. More money to people suing? How is that a problem for others who might sue? As a result of these payments, the leads might not have looked out for the best interests of the entire class, as they are supposed to do, but instead worked on their own behalf.

Lerach and Weiss asserted that these payments were simply business-as-usual in the class action game, and that turns out to be the greatest problem. It's tough to take the high road, scolding corporations for mishandling the funds of investors, when you are doing patently illegal and underhanded things on the plaintiff side. Prosecutors say the Milberg firm paid secret kickbacks to plaintiffs in more than 165 lawsuits over 25 years that earned the firm nearly $240 million in legal fees. In a recent magazine article done while in the slammer, Lerach admitted, "Paying plaintiffs was an industry practice."

Lerach is looking at two years in prison and a fine of $7.75 million. Weiss was required to pay a fine of $9.8 million, and was sentenced to 30 months. Under an agreement with prosecutors, the firm itself will pay a $75 million fine—one of the largest ever against a law firm—and the government will ask a court to dismiss an indictment of the firm, which has reorganized under the simpler name, Milberg.

Cases like these poison the well and give ammunition to politicians who want to impose tougher standards on shareholder claims. Judges wonder if other lawyers who do this work are also crooked. And the courts impose higher standards on shareholder suits than ever before. All of this hurts your efforts to find justice.

Hold to a Higher Standard

Lawyers can make mistakes and some deadlines get missed. It is unfortunate, but true. But the least a client can expect from his attorney is that he will follow the law. When we can't trust legal counsel to act in a lawful manner, the system goes haywire. A fiduciary breach or an ethical lapse by a professional can hit you where it hurts. But the stakes rise anytime law enforcement enters the fray.

Size dictates the amount of their criminal sin, particularly when involving white-collar crime. An accountant who embezzles $20,000 from someone's retirement funds will earn his comeuppance. But if that same accountant takes 20 wealthy clients for a total of $40 million, the level of interest by prosecutors naturally peaks. In either case, expect the law to grind toward justice and for some crimes to garner more attention than others. And as in the case involving the Milberg lawyers, we can all feel cheated by criminal actions.

For those wronged by a professional who goes astray, the legal system may provide the only avenue for redress. In most cases, waiting for a legal intervention to happen out of the blue can take a long time. Authorities may identify lawbreakers during regular investigations, but most cases break when someone files a complaint or volunteers some information. With many white-collar felonies, a grand jury hears the testimony and decides if enough evidence exists to send a case to trial. At other times, a prosecutor can make a unilateral decision to proceed.

The grand jury structure varies by state, with about half of all states requiring a grand jury indictment before the trial of a felony case. In other states, a grand jury might have the power to bring felony charges, but prosecutors can make a decision to use this panel or not.

When is turning to the criminal justice system worthwhile? In most cases, the filing of charges does not help you as much as it helps the state. But when someone commits a crime, punishment should follow. You should take your responsibility as a good citizen seriously and do what you can to help. Your actions may prevent someone else from falling victim, and you have to admit that the flush of revenge you feel from putting the bad guys away can be sweet indeed.

In some cases, though, you can actually benefit from helping to catch the bad guy. A court might order restitution, which requires a criminal to reimburse victims for financial damages. Most states have laws allowing restitution, but not all states enforce the rules. Federal courts routinely require it, but there is no guarantee the guilty will still possess the money to pay.

A downside to filing criminal charges rather than a lawsuit in civil court is a loss of control over the matter. Civil lawsuits are between you and the other person. Criminal charges, though, are filed by the state or federal authority against someone else. You can only assist the prosecution in the matter. The prosecutor may ask your opinion about the criminal penalties being offered in a plea bargain, but only the authorities have the power to make the deal.

You also can't use the threat of criminal charges to affect a civil settlement in your favor without risking charges yourself. This is called misprision of a felony, which means that you are aware of the commission of a crime and fail to report it, and even try to profit from not reporting it.

Deciding to Call The Law

When it comes to white-collar crime, victims often fail to realize what is happening until too much time passes. You should take care to recognize the warnings when they appear, says Ted Steinke, who spent 18 years as a prosecutor in the Dallas District Attorney's office. He specialized in white-collar crime, commercial fraud and professional misconduct. As a private attorney, he often works with individuals, corporations and government entities to help them present cases to law enforcement involving criminal misconduct.

In any potential case, the first step requires recognizing a crime. "Let's say that you invested money with an investment advisor and you're not satisfied with the way he's handled the money," Steinke says. "Just because you are not satisfied does not mean he's done something criminal."

The laws in play typically focus on fiduciary duty, spelling out the specifics of the legal responsibilities inherent in someone who handles the money or financial future of others. For example, in some states each partner in a two-person partnership owns 100% of a business. If one partner takes control of the business cash, like what happened to C.L. Nathanson in Chapter 7, theft laws would not apply. No one can steal what he or she already owns, even if the move leaves the other partner high and dry. Instead, laws governing fiduciary duty come into play. Because C.L. was destitute, she went after the money first. In some instances, victims will file criminal charges first or file criminal charges and a civil lawsuit at the same time. Most states have similar laws, providing legal tools for the courts and law enforcement to navigate complex disagreements and financial scams.

Regardless of the specific laws, the first step is to identify when a crime occurs. For many people, scams and schemes often appear in the form of investments, requiring you to spot when a deal slips off the tracks.

"There are certain red flags and individuals need to be aware that they may indicate some kind of criminal conduct. And by criminal conduct, I'm talking about actually stealing the money or doing something with it other than what you agreed to do," Steinke says.

Warning Signs

Few instances of white-collar crime happen without some warning. The signs that things might not be quite right are as follows:

- A broker, accountant or other fiduciary stops returning phone calls. You visit the fiduciary's office. If no one is there, you have every right to be concerned.
- Attempts to send e-mail or regular mail fail to elicit a response. Send a certified letter, which if returned unopened also indicates a possible scam in play.
- Pay attention to the correspondence you receive, particularly

statements about how your money was used. For example, your broker agreed to put your money into a low-risk mutual fund but you start to receive updates about a high-risk investment in venture-funded technology companies. Sometimes the misdeed is that obvious.

- A broker fails to provide monthly statements or any evidence that he or she actually invested your money.

Any explanation you get about your money should make sense. It's incredible how gullible we can be. Alan Funt, who produced and starred in that famous early television show, *Candid Camera*, was constantly amazed at what excuses people would believe. When someone he hoped to fool would walk into a room, there might be a large camera in the corner with a sheet draped over it. He would simply tell the person it was part of the ventilation system or some other lie and go on his way. Rarely would anyone question his explanation.

Meeting With the Police

When someone steals from you, the response seems obvious: call the police. Often, however, the reality is more complex. Where you live, the amounts involved and how you present the case make a difference.

"If you are in a small town where the police and the local prosecutors have limited resources," Steinke says, "they may not be able to handle a sophisticated fraud case as quickly or as well as a larger police agency or a larger district attorney's office."

Even in large cities, the size of staffs and resources assigned to handle white-collar crimes varies by jurisdiction. For example, some district attorneys assign teams to investigate and prosecute the cases, while other DAs only handle the prosecution and leave investigations to police.

As a result, the response to white-collar crime is inconsistent. Often an individual who believes he's been defrauded will call the police, who tell him this is a civil case and he needs to contact a lawyer.

Preparing for the Worst

No one enters a business deal anticipating a crime, but you should anticipate and prepare for misdeeds. Ramp up your record collecting and note taking when the red flags appear.

Copy all cancelled checks, both front and back, and keep the copies in your records. Focus on checks written to stockbrokers, lawyers or any other professional to whom you trusted money.

Maintain all of your financial records in an orderly manner. In a case of financial fraud, you must show damages, and detailed record keeping can offer a key resource to illustrate your losses.

Collect and file any promotional material such as brochures or direct mail pieces you receive regarding an investment or other financial agreement. If the deal goes bad, prosecutors will want to see evidence of the promises made and how the reality differed from the ads.

Maintain copies of all correspondence, whether e-mail or regular mail. If you begin to question a financial agreement, the broker or other professional will often start making excuses. Records of these excuses, and the possible contradictions contained in them, can aid prosecutors.

Once you realize something is amiss, prepare the items a prosecutor will require. Begin by constructing a chronology, including the dates and times of meetings and conversations.

Write down detailed notes of everything the perpetrator said during meetings, including any promises made or excuses provided. Well-ordered notes can show your credibility.

If possible, use an Excel spreadsheet to summarize any payments to the perpetrator. Put the spreadsheet on a CD and submit it with the case. This offers an easy way for authorities to have an overview of your losses.

Hiring a Lawyer to Prompt a Police Response

"If a consumer contacts a lawyer first to get an opinion as to whether there is a crime,' says Steinke, "the lawyer can go one step further and present the case to law enforcement so that it's not that difficult to understand. A lot of times, a lawyer can spend three or four hours and put a case together that is much more attractive to law enforcement than if the victim just brought in a bunch of documents that were not properly collated and prepared."

A lawyer will normally charge by the hour to prepare the case, requiring from three to four hours for a basic case and as many as 20 hours or more for complex issues demanding witness interviews and explanations of intricate business situations.

"I really feel that when someone calls and they're not prepared to talk law enforcement language about the specific statues that have been violated, they get the cold shoulder from the police," Steinke says. "Law enforcement has an easy response. They are in the business of investigating murders, rapes and robberies, and they think you've got a civil deal. It's an easy and effective way for law enforcement to not get involved in cases that very likely might end up being civil in nature after all."

Not all cases require the aid of an attorney. Most police departments assign officers to handle situations such as identity theft or credit card fraud. You do not need an attorney to help present these cases, Steinke says.

When it comes to sophisticated fraud, however, presenting a well-defined case to police is important. Consider a neighbor who befriends an elderly woman and targets her as a mark for a scam. The neighbor encourages the woman to rewrite her will and allow the neighbor to make bank withdrawals. The woman's money disappears until her out-of-town relatives realize the scam.

When the relatives approach the police, law enforcement might at first consider this a civil case focused on whether or not the woman legally provided her consent to the neighbor. A lawyer, though, might be able to put together the details and point out how the neighbor broke specific criminal statutes.

Timing and Venue

When it comes to approaching law enforcement, deciding whom to contact first represents a key strategic choice. Going to the authorities, having the case rejected and then seeking a lawyer to help might not always work.

"If they turn a case down once, they'll turn it down again, even if it's packaged properly," Steinke says. Rejecting and then later resurrecting a case might embarrass authorities, often leading them to simply drop the matter.

Choosing the proper venue is also a critical choice. Steinke says that when working with corporations, he often determines if federal authorities have jurisdiction. "Sometimes you can get the investigation done quicker on the federal level, but there's also a financial consideration," he says. In one case, a company lost $350,000 in a wire transfer scheme, but the local FBI office turned it down because not enough money was lost. Instead, state lawmakers prosecuted the case.

In instances such as when a broker draws victims from several counties for an investment scheme, your attorney might seek out the county with the district attorney best equipped to guide a case to prosecution.

Even when you are the victim of a crime, it often pays to define a strategy before contacting police.

23

Scams for Today and Tomorrow

Two young kids of the Great Depression came together in uncertain times with thoughts of hearth and home. They were more fortunate than most, being among the few couples they knew who both earned college degrees. He was an engineer and took a job with the railroad. Her passion was teaching, and she was devoted to her elementary school. They lived a comfortable life, raised two kids and realized the American Dream. By no means were they wealthy, except in those intangibles that make life a joy.

By the time they reached retirement age, he had his workshop behind the garage. She was a school principal with a wide social network. Their home was paid for on a beautiful tree-lined street, and they spent some of their hard-earned money traveling the world. Now that young man has passed away, his bride is in her nineties, and a curious thing has happened.

She is going to leave her children an inheritance of more than two million dollars. They built up that nest egg through hard work. They nursed it with frugal living. And they kept it by conservative investing.

Only in this way could two Depression-era kids with middle-class jobs amass an estate worth more money than they could ever imagine.

Their frugality is legend within the family. Younger members of the family just shake their heads in a kind of perplexed wonder that the old folks never put their money into "something that would really grow." Their caution is a by-product of the extreme economic conditions that gripped that generation. Because of their lifestyle and the conditions of their upbringing, they have an inheritance to leave their children, grand-children and great grandchildren.

And there is one thing more, perhaps the most important reason. They were easily able to regulate their greed, for with this generation of Americans greed was not clever or desired. It caused you to do stupid things with your money, while they knew the best policy was to leave the money in safe investments—muncipal bonds and passbook savings —gaining slight interest and growing the money over the decades.

Replicate this scene many times over and you have a remarkable oc-currence – the largest transfer of wealth from one generation to another in history, an estimated $41 trillion-dollar windfall for the Baby Boom-ers. Along with the money comes a genuine concern that the inheriting generation doesn't know how to handle the windfall and will wind up squandering it or losing it to charlatans.

And in many cases they will be right. That greatest generation, which endured World War II and deprivation, is one of savers and hoarders, while the boomer generation is one of consumers and spenders. Conser-vative municipal bonds came of age with the older folks, while wildly flaky junk bonds are a product of today's middle-agers.

There is every reason to suspect that boomers who inherit all this wealth will be prime targets for those who rob at pen point. All that money burning holes in the pockets of those who would take a risk for a higher return may bring about the next big series of scams.

A Nation of Concentrated Wealth

The transfer of wealth through inheritance has contributed to the increasing concentration of wealth in our society.

In 2005, the highest-earning one percent of Americans brought home at least $348,000, with some earning much, much more. The number of households with a net worth of at least $1 million—excluding the value of the family home itself—increased 5.9 percent between 2006 and 2007.

For thousands of Americans, a practical reality exists. People die and income tied up in businesses, investments and bank accounts, the very money often responsible for the income gap, must be distributed. And the methods of distribution often follow the debates and arguments swirling around economic fairness that contributed to the election of Barack Obama.

Some people opt for charitable solutions. In 2006, Warren Buffett, 75 years old at the time and still the brain behind Berkshire Hathaway, announced plans for his $40 billion fortune.

He promised to give 85% of his Berkshire Hathaway stock to five foundations. The bulk of it is going to the Bill & Melinda Gates Foundation, a charitable trust with programs to fight world-wide health problems as well as improve education in the United States. Who could argue, except possibly Buffett's children? He earned my respect when he famously said that he wanted to leave his children enough money that they could do something, but not enough that they could do nothing.

One critical part of this transfer of money through inheritance is the great amount that will go to charitable causes, as much as $6 trillion over the next half-century. This is real money, destined to get the creative juices flowing of those who steal for a living. The scams and con jobs of today will pale by comparison to those in the future. And like our approach to terrorism or other threats, we are always preparing for the last attack while the enemy is planning something completely new.

Probably the best we can do is not wave large bills around to show our economic status, but to rely on the structure of trusts to offer some protection.

Trusts

In the end, no one escapes their mortality, although people often put off planning for the inevitable. Who will manage the estate? Is there enough money set aside for the children? Who has the wisdom and honesty to manage the remaining assets? Ask one tough question and others follow. For those with significant assets, creation of a trust offers an option to protect long-term assets and ensure distribution of assets in a specific manner set out at the trust's creation.

In a trust, you define the person you wish to manage your assets. You set the rules, even establishing how, or if, your heirs can replace the trust manager. You can limit how assets are invested, such as prohibiting investment in startup businesses, junk bonds and close friends. You can choose how and when your heirs receive money from the trust, and what money can be used for other purchases, such as education, health care or the accumulation of certain assets. When heirs are minor children, a trust can take the financial responsibility off the children's guardian, allowing an independent party to focus on the best interest of the minor.

Creation of a trust can ease complications at the time of death, when the family must cope with so much: funeral, family and mourning. Unlike the probate of a will, an established trust does not require a judge's approval.

When it comes time to craft a trust, many options exist. Someone might create a living trust, setting aside the money and managing the assets themselves until they die, when the trust might become irrevocable. An irrevocable trust establishes the particulars of a trust and cannot be changed. A charitable remainder unitrust can distribute money to charity while also creating a tax advantage to remaining beneficiaries. Also, a testamentary trust can manage assets destined for beneficiaries.

The key feature of any trust is that the person creating the trust gives up a certain amount of control of their money during their lifetime. It is possible to tailor a trust to the specific needs and circumstances of an individual, which adds complexity, the potential for confusion and the possibility of angry benefactors. Always seek out an attorney or financial manager who specializes in trusts.

A Broken Trust

Take family. Add money. The result is often a nasty equation filled with animosity. With emotions high, arguments over family money rarely depend on the dollar amount. Some families can square off over just a few thousand dollars or the fate of an antique couch. At other times, long-running battles over cash land in court.

Few cases reach the heights of the Pritzker family, one of Chicago's wealthiest. A Jewish emigrant from Kiev, Nicholas Pritzker laid the foundation for the empire in the 1880s. As the legend goes, he taught himself English by reading the newspaper, eventually becoming a lawyer.

Over more than 125 years, the Pritzker wealth grew to $15 billion, including the Hyatt hotel chain, dozens of companies beneath the umbrella of the Marmon Group and 2,500 trusts, many of which funded charities. Then, in 2005, details of an internal battle surfaced. Liesel Pritzker, an actress who starred as a child in movies such as *Air Force One* and *The Little Princess*, and her brother, Matthew, sued their family members.

They accused their father, Robert Pritzker, of robbing his children's trust funds during his divorce from their mother. And the suit increased the stakes of a separate family business move, a legal agreement by 11 cousins to divide the family's assets.

The case never went to trial, reaching a 2008 settlement that gave $900 million to the brother and sister, including an immediate $280 million payout. Imagine attending a family holiday gathering after such a fight.

And the Pritzker family is far from being alone.

A Shifting Trust

When establishing a trust, one of the critical choices is the selection of the trustee, the person who will manage the assets. Many factors govern this option-filled choice, and a consultation with a good estate attorney can offer guidance. Beware, however, if the lawyer drafting the trust document also wants to be the trustee. A fundamental change in crafting a trust shifted the burden of responsibility and raised the family stakes.

Traditionally, someone creating a trust chooses his or her local bank's trust department as a third party to handle the assets, says Kathy Muldoon, vice president of Carter Financial Management. Beginning in the 1980s, though, bank mergers gobbled up many hometown banks and the choices of trustee, the person or persons charged with managing the trust, shrank dramatically. Rather than depend on an institution whose top managers lived in another city, many people looked elsewhere for a trustee.

Estate lawyers started suggesting using family members as trustees, a hedge against a bank's ownership change or dissatisfaction with a bank's management of the funds, Muldoon says.

As a result, many of these decisions made in the 1980s by the parents of the baby boom generation have now come into play, leaving boomers to contend with the financial structures established by their parents.

For these now aging boomers, the responsibility can be great. Not all parents, for example, even tell their children of the trust provisions or that one child will manage the assets for the rest of the family.

Hard feelings are only one possible result. Managing a trust creates a legal responsibility to follow the demands created by the trust, but avoiding trouble can be as simple as open discussion and full disclosure among family members. Muldoon believes family meetings are essential, allowing everyone to understand the basics of the trust. Also, in this example, the parents should explain to the children the actions taken to form a trust and the reasons for those actions. The goal is simple: avoid surprises regarding a family member's role in a trust or the size of the assets.

Taking the role of trustee creates a powerful responsibility. This person carries a fiduciary duty, a legal obligation to put the trust's well being above his or her own.

As a result, the trustee should have an attorney walk them through the documents and legal requirements of the role. The trustee must not only adhere to the instructions defined in the original trust documents, but also prudently manage the trusts and distribution. "Along the way, there's massive opportunity for mistakes," Muldoon says. At times sorting out right from wrong can prove difficult.

The family of Mary Kay Ash, who brought the world pink Cadillacs and neighborhood cosmetics sales, turned ugly in a dispute following her death. Kathlyn Kerr, one of Ash's granddaughters, sued the Bank of America and her uncle, Richard Rogers, who co-founded Mary Kay with Ash in 1969. Kerr wanted to boot them out as trustees of the family trust funds, a fortune worth nearly $98 million.

Rogers, the sole trustee, denied wrongdoing and accused Kerr of basic greed. The contention involved multiple trusts, family tension and questions of the management of the funds. Kerr argued that too much of the money remained invested in Mary Kay, Inc., rather than in a more diversified portfolio.

Kerr's family, meanwhile, was not destitute. Far from it. Payments from trusts created by Ash were about $350,000 annually, and the fund paid for her children's education. Between 2001 and 2006, she received more than $2 million from the family trust.

For a more typical family, Muldoon believes basic guidelines can help a family manage a trust in an equitable manner. Unless he or she is also a lawyer, a trustee should hire good estate counsel to explain the intent and scope of duties, including the limitations and distribution requirements. With a range of possible trusts, such as those that protect the wealth of a minor child, attention to detail is critical.

Manage the trust in a manner that adheres to the original trust document's wishes. For example, a trust might have been designed to support a beneficiary's education or as a hedge against illness and health-related bills. Failing to follow set guidelines to meet these goals can expose the trustee to litigation.

Remember that in a trust you are always dealing with other people's money. Typically, funds in a trust are invested, and the trust documents can define the scope of those investments. To limit the potential risk of loss, a trust can be designed to prohibit investment in commodities, land deals or speculative companies. The specifics are unique to each trust. While the trust documents define what is permitted, the trustee has the job of managing the trust in accordance with guidelines that include the accepted approach to the use of capital.

Do the beneficiaries have any recourse if they suspect mismanagement? Often, they may. A trust can also specify the circumstances in which a trustee can be removed, often an important issue if a bank or someone outside a family manages the assets. A trust might allow a vote by two of three beneficiaries to remove a trustee. Each trust is different. Always seek professional aid in structuring a trust. No one wants to face the anger and division seen in instances such as the Pritzker or Mary Kay families.

Can You Make Your Future Scam-Free?

We've covered many of the ways professionals can rob you at pen point. We've talked about the remedies for such injustices and how to recover some (if not all) of your money.

We could talk about how you grieve if you can't make a recovery, but we will leave that to the individual. I am concerned for those who were not successful with anything we suggested. For them I ask, "Is life really over if you don't recover the money you lost?" In most cases, people tell me their lives are still good, the sun comes up in the morning, and their children and spouse still love them.

Any attorney who practices in this field gets a strong feeling of why we do this work and how successful we can be for our client. The biggest case I ever had gave me that feeling, that being allowed to work against those who rob at pen point is a gift in itself. It involved one of the first families of Mexico, which does business in this country and Europe, as well as their own country. This was no ordinary investment. They had determined that they had too much money invested in their own country, and they felt sure it would be safe across the border.

This was the mid-1980s, and they made connections with a stockbroker who would shepherd their money through the system. They were not greedy for high returns. They specifically instructed the broker that they wanted to keep their original investment intact and ready in case they needed to withdraw the money on short notice. They didn't want him to do anything risky with their principal.

Over the course of almost five years, the family invested about $30 million with the broker. At first, their account was on the up-and-up. He invested the money wisely and sent this family the standard reports generated by the brokerage firm. Each quarter, he traveled to Mexico to offer a review of their position, summarized in his own reports.

Then came the stock market crash of 1987 and the broker panicked. With everyone losing money, including the broker personally, he felt the need to "balance out" the accounts – and lie about doing it. He became more secretive about this account, tracking it closely each day and churning it at the end of the month to show activity and generate commissions. He wouldn't let anyone in the firm have access to the account information and even generated his own reports.

On paper, the account appeared to be making money and everything seemed okay. Then came the call that the broker always dreaded. The Mexican government was taking the national telephone company public, and the country's president asked the family to help the process along by purchasing a huge chunk of stock. They needed their money.

Now the broker and his company were in trouble. After several months of dodging their entreaties, the broker sent them a small portion of their investment and no one could explain why that was the case.

These are gracious, genteel people, but they were determined to get to the bottom of this. That's when they hired me and my partner to recover the money from the broker and his firm.

Although the case was exceedingly clear cut, it took months to get the full scope of the broker's fraud. We worked the case as if it would go to trial, but it was apparent that the case would settle. The downside was too great for the brokerage house. And in the end, although the broker absconded with a large share of the investment, we were able to recover almost 90% of the family's money. When I discussed the meaning of this case with members of this family, I knew we were on the side of the angels.

"We never thought this could happen to us in the United States," said the elder son. "We brought our money here because everyone knows this is the safest place for it in the world. In Mexico and in other countries we expect thievery, but not here."

By recovering this money, we did our small part to rebuild the confidence these investors had lost in our market system. The brokers, the lawyers and the other professionals we call on account for their deeds owe a debt of gratitude to cases like this one.

Through the various means available in the American civil justice system, we are able to convince investors and businesspeople to continue their participation simply by brushing back those who rob at pen point.

Acknowledgments

No one person ever completes a project like this by himself, and so I want to thank a few people who helped me tell this tale.

Foremost among these is my law partner, Robert Tobey, who does such a good job attending to details while I dwell on the big picture. Robert has offered many good suggestions about the direction the book has taken.

The rest of our staff, including my legal assistant, Michelle Spear, has been helpful compiling the case work that went into the manuscript. Several of my children read parts of the book and offered insightful comments that helped overall presentation.

The people at my publisher, PSG Books, have gone the extra mile to make the book as authoritative as possible. Researcher and writer Noble Sprayberry helped to flesh out my concept. My editor, Larry Upshaw, has spent more time than he ever imagined making the book as palatable as possible to a wide range of injured people while still retaining my voice.

Glossary
of Professional Malpractice Terms

Adversary system – The adversary system is the shorthand used to describe the American judicial process for arriving at truth. In its simplest form, it means that the two sides to a dispute each hire a lawyer and that the lawyers then go at each other, each side doing their very best to put forward the best case possible for their respective client, while the judge and jury watches the process and then decides the winner. A lack of understanding of the fundamentals of the adversary process is one of the reasons the public thinks lawyers will say anything for money. What they don't understand is that the lawyer's job is to advance his client's interest passionately, within the rules, without regard to the lawyer's personal opinion, so that a judge or jury can then resolve the dispute after having heard both sides. The biggest flaw in the adversary system is, of course, when one lawyer fails to do a good job.

Advertising review – The bar associations in an increasing number of states are instituting advertising review to approves television ads, Web sites and other forms of attorney and law firm solicitation media.

Alternative Dispute Resolution (ADR) – In its broadest form, any alternative to the court room as a means of resolving a dispute. Arbitration and mediation are the most common forms, but others include summary jury trials, focus groups, collaborative law, Christian counseling, etc.

Annuity – A contract, usually with an insurance company, under which you pay a lump sum of money and the company pays you back in regular payments with some amount of interest. Many annuities provide lifetime payments, so that if you die young, the insurance company stops payments and makes a profit, but if you live a long life, the insurance company loses money because of how long the payments last.

Apology laws – These are laws designed to permit one party of the other in a lawsuit to apologize for their behavior without having their apology used as evidence against them in a lawsuit.

Appellate attorney – An attorney who specializes in handling an appeal after a trial. It is not unusual for them to have some role during the trial, to ensure that the trial lawyer takes the appropriate steps to preserve legal disputes for the appeal, but most of their work is done after the trial and consists of writing the appellate brief and arguing to the court of appeals.

Arbitration – A form of Alternative Dispute Resolution created by contract. Essentially, the parties agree not to go to court and have any disputes resolved by a private trial. The procedures in arbitration are determined by the contract. Businesses like arbitration because they are afraid that a jury will enter a huge award against them and they believe that an arbitrator will not.

Asset management – Also known as wealth or money managers, they decide how investor money will be allocated.

Auditor – Usually a CPA, this professional goes into a company and checks to be sure that the things the company is saying about their finances are true. These people are sometimes called "bean counters."

AV rating – This is the highest rating given to a lawyer by the Martindale Hubbell publications. It is supposed to be reserved for a small percentage of the lawyers in any one community, but there are a lot of AV rated lawyers out there making serious mistakes.

Bailiff – Usually a member of the local sheriff's department, this is a person whose job it is to maintain order in the courtroom. If the court holds you in contempt, it is the bailiff that will take you to jail.

Bonds – Bonds come in all types, shapes and sizes. A bond is essentially an investment vehicle in which you pay a certain amount of money in return for the promise to be paid back more money than you paid in. Bonds tend to be more secure than equity investments, such as shares in a corporation, but the downside is that the maximum amount you can make from your investment is predetermined and will not increase, no matter how well the issue of the bond does financially.

Bonds, junk – This a term coined in the '80s for bonds issued usually by corporate undercapitalized corporations or start up businesses. As a result, the bonds are much more risky than the high rated bonds issues by governments or large corporations. In return for that increased risk, however, junk bonds usually have a higher rate of return to compensate for their higher rate of failure.

Bonds, municipal – Whenever a governmental entity wants to make a large capital purchase, such as a county that wants to build a new bridge, the entity issues bonds that they sell to individuals to finance the building project. In essence, those who purchase the bonds are loaning money to the entity.

Certified financial planner – A person who has gone through the licensing procedure and received the Certified Financial Planner designation. The CFP designation is at least some evidence that the person who wants to tell you what to do with your money has undergone training and has education on the subject. Like every other designation, however, it is not a guarantee that you won't be robbed at pen point.

Certified public accountant – This is an accountant who has taken and passed an elaborate CPA examination in his/her state and has agreed to abide by certain rules, regulations and guidelines issued by the various state CPA organizations. While the dividing line on a CPA's loyalty is sometimes disputed, it is generally considered that a certified public accountant owes some professional duty to the public at large and not just to his or her clients.

Churning – This a colorful term used to describe the activity of a stockbroker who buys and sells stock for his client (earning a commission on every buy and every sale) for the purpose of increasing his commissions as opposed to the purpose of generating sound investments for his client. To determine whether a stockbroker has engaged in churning, lawyers look at such things as earnings to balance ratios and turnover ratios.

Class action – This is a lawsuit in which one person brings a lawsuit on behalf of an entire group of people similarly situated. If, for example, a bank routinely rounds the interest in your account down to the nearest penny, a class action might be a good device to address that wrong, since no one person would have damages large enough to justify a lawsuit even though the bank could be profiting millions of dollars.

Clear and convincing evidence – This is one of several legal descriptions for the burden of proof required for a plaintiff to win a lawsuit. Most civil cases require a plaintiff to prove her case by a preponderance of the evidence, which is generally described as anything over 50%. Criminal trials require proof beyond a reasonable doubt, which is a much higher standard and is often described as that standard of persuasion that you would require in order to make decisions on the most important affairs of your life. The clear and convincing standard is someone between the preponderance and the beyond a reasonable doubt standard and is usually reserved for issues related to exemplary damages or other claims where courts or the legislature have decided that more proof should be required than a mere preponderance of the evidence.

Collaborative law – Collaborative law is best understood when it is contrasted with the adversary system, defined above. The concept of collaborative law is that, rather than declaring war on each other, the parties to a dispute will, with their lawyers, engage in a process of trying to resolve the matter more amicably. The process is extremely well suited to family law disputes involving children as any one who remembers the movie Kramer v. Kramer would attest.

Commercial law – This is a catch-all phrase generally used to describe any aspect of the law involving business transactions.

Confidentiality – Lawyers are required to keep all of the information they learn about and from their clients confidential pursuant to their ethical obligations. Occasionally, at the end of a dispute, however, an additional obligation of "confidentiality" is imposed as a term of settlement. Why confidentiality agreements serve very useful purposes in some cases, most of the time they should be resisted.

Contingent fee – In its simplest form, contingent fee means that a lawyer does not get paid unless he wins. This is an alternative way to pay your lawyer instead of paying the lawyer by the hour. The theory is that because the lawyer is at risk of receiving no payment, he will receive more than his normal hourly rate if he wins, thus making up for those cases he takes on a contingent fee and doesn't win. Originally in plaintiff's personal injury cases, the contingent fee is finding much broader application today in commercial litigation, although a contingent fee is generally illegal in family law and criminal law matters.

Cost of living – As we all know, prices change every year, usually going up. The "cost of living index" is the government's attempt to quantify how much money you have to make this year to live exactly the same way you lived last year. Inflation is obviously a big part of the cost of living, but it is not synonymous with the cost of living.

Court clerk – Every court has an employee whose job is to keep track of the mountains of paper that come in on a daily basis. That person is the court clerk. Most of the time, the court clerk is also the representative of the court who schedules hearings and trials, although some courts use a court coordinator for that job. One lesson every young lawyer should learn is to never make the court clerk angry.

Court reporter – This person's job is to keep an accurate written record of everything that happens in the courtroom. Today, most court reporting is done with a stenography machine, a little larger than a shoe box, in which she types symbols that are then converted into written text. The reporter usually sits in front of the judge near the witness stand, so she can hear.

Court, appeals – Every state's judicial system is divided into trial courts and appellate courts. While the names are different from state to state, the trial courts are, quite obviously, where the trials actually take place. Juries are impaneled, witnesses are questioned and cross-examined, and lawyers make impassioned closing arguments and then one side wins and one side loses. After the trial is over, the parties to the lawsuit have the opportunity to appeal the outcome of the trial to an appellate court. These courts of appeals are charged with responsibility for ensuring that there are no mistakes made in the trial court. That is not the same, however, as making sure that the right result was reached. An appeal is not a second bite at the apple and in two-thirds of all appeals, the decision of the original trial court is left untouched.

Court, civil – Some states have courts of general jurisdiction that handle every kind of dispute. Urban areas with larger populations, however, often have specialized courts that handle only certain types of cases. The most common division of courts is criminal courts, civil courts, and family courts.

Court, criminal – In the criminal courts, the party bringing the lawsuit is the state (or federal government), and they are represented by a government employee, usually in the district attorney's office. The defendant will be one of your fellow citizens or a corporation and the object of the criminal court is to determine whether the defendant committed a crime and, if so, what punishment is appropriate.

Court, family – Family law courts handle divorces, annulments and issues related to children such as paternity, custody, visitation, and child support.

Court, juvenile – Juvenile courts handle criminal complaints brought by the state against individuals under the age of 18, based upon the assumption (which no one who has had children could dispute) that children should be treated differently than adults because they often make mistakes just because their brains are not fully developed or they don't have sufficient life experience to make good decisions, as opposed to having purposefully decided to do a bad act. Unfortunately, however, the current trend is to try more and more children as adults. See Chapter 2, where Senator John Cornyn complained because the U.S. Supreme Court would not let Texas execute a minor.

Court, supreme – In most states, the highest court is called the supreme court (although, in New York, they actually have a trial court that is called a supreme court). The state supreme court is above the court of appeals and is on most matters the court of last resort. Many supreme courts have what is called discretionary review, which means they do not have to take an appeal, but can pick and chose and, therefore, only take those cases where they think their decision will affect the entire state, such as correcting a misinterpretation of the law. Sadly, in those states that have discretionary supreme courts, the highest court in the state doesn't even care whether you got a fair trial and a proper result, unless your case somehow affects the entire state you live in.

Courts, federal – The federal government maintains a judicial system that consists of three levels of court; the district courts, which are trial courts; 11 courts of appeals, divided by geographic area; and the U.S. Supreme Court, which is a discretionary supreme court. Federal courts handle disputes involving federal law (such as admiralty and federal securities law violations) as well as some disputes between citizens of different states, what is called diversity of citizenship.

Courts, bankruptcy – The U.S. Government maintains a series of bankruptcy courts whose job is to administer the affairs of and resolve disputes involving persons and corporations who file for bankruptcy. The affairs of a bankruptcy court involve strictly administrative matters, such as determining who will run a bankrupt company and how much money can be paid to lawyers representing the company as well as litigation matters, such as trying lawsuits involving claims for or against the bankrupt person or corporation.

Crash – A market crash is a precipitous drop in the stock market (usually occurring in one or two days). The most drastic crash was April 29, 1929, which began the Great Depression. We also had serious market crashes in October 1987 and October 1999. The current market decline is technically not a "crash" because it is taking so long for the market to drop and because it is not wholly unexpected, although to the people losing money it really doesn't matter.

Damage model – Damage model is simply the elements and methodology used to calculate your loses in any dispute. It could include such elements as loss of principle on an investment, interest on the money lost, lost profit on a product you were unable to sell or loss of business reputation as a result of having purchased contaminated product for your manufactured goods. One of your lawyer's jobs is to prepare and present on your behalf a persuasive and compelling damage model that includes all of the elements of damage that you could reasonably expect to recover.

Defendant – In a civil trial, the defendant is the person being sued by the plaintiff. In a criminal court, the defendant is the person against whom criminal charges have been brought by the state.

Deposition – A deposition is recorded testimony that can be used in a civil trial the same as live testimony. Depositions are typically taken in a lawyer's office, with both sides present, with a court reporter there to transcribe all of the questions and answers. Depositions may also be videotaped. Typically, there are no depositions permitted in arbitration or in criminal trials.

Disclaimer – A written notice that the seller or manufacturer of a product does not intent to stand behind a product if you feel harmed by it. Disclaimers are routinely put on every product today, even though courts often refuse to enforce them. Do not let a disclaimer discourage you from consulting with an attorney, who can then advise you on whether the disclaimer will be enforced or not.

Discovery – After decades of "trial by ambush," the court system determined that lawsuits would go better if both sides where forced to disclose information about the case. The tools by which you can compel the other side to disclose information are referred generally as discovery and consist of such things as depositions, interrogatories, requests to produce documents, and request for admissions.

Dividends – Money paid by a corporation to its shareholders, its owners. As an owner of the business, you're entitled to a share of the profits. Unfortunately, in recent years, dividends have dried up as corporations pay their profit to their CEOs and investors look to increased stock prices to justify their investment instead of dividends. If you receive a dividend payment, it is income to you and is taxable.

Duty – Duty is the legal concept that describes the behavior we owe to each other. When you are driving your car, you owe a duty to every person on the street to operate your vehicle in a safe and reasonable manner. The duty is generally described as the conduct of the "ordinary prudent person/lawyer/doctor/stockbroker, under the same or similar circumstances."

Duty, breach of – A professional breaches his duty, and therefore commits an act of negligence, when he or she fails to act in accordance with the conduct of the mythical ordinary prudent person under the same or similar circumstances. For example, the ordinary prudent attorney would file a lawsuit on time, before limitations run. Failure to file the lawsuit on time, resulting in the lawsuit being dismissed, would usually breach the duty that the lawyer owes to the client.

Estate planner – As applied to the legal profession, an estate planner is a lawyer who specializes in helping people structure their wealth, both for their lifetime and upon their death. Estate planners are typically extremely well versed in tax laws (especially the estate tax) and can help their clients implement numerous strategies to legally minimize the taxes they owe upon their death. Estate planners are also a group of lawyers who draft and prepare wills and trust documents for clients.

Equities – This is a term used to describe ownership in a company through shares of stock. Most financial planners think of investments in terms of equities and bonds, with equities being riskier but having greater chance of high return and bonds being more secure but having their return limited by contract.

Expert witness – An expert witness is a person who, typically, has no first hand knowledge of the dispute that is permitted to testify to his or her opinions. An expert witness could testify, for example, that the interaction of two drugs in a person could induce brain damage. Expert witnesses have to be qualified by way of education and/or experience before the court will permit their testimony. In virtually every malpractice case, an expert witness is required to testify to the breach of duty by the defendant professional.

Federal Deposit Insurance Corporation (FDIC) – This is the federally funded corporation that stands behind and guarantees the deposits of banks. The FDIC limit of its guarantee was previously $100,000, although that limit was raised to $250,000 with the "bailout" legislation passed by the U.S. Congress and signed by President Bush in late 2008.

Fiduciary duty – This is the highest duty recognized by the law and it requires that a person put the interests of another before his or her own interests. Officers of a corporation, for example, owe a fiduciary duty to the corporation and are supposed to look out for the best interest of the corporation and not their own best interests. Lawyers, likewise, owe a fiduciary duty to clients.

Frivolous lawsuit – This is someone else's lawsuit. When Mrs. Brown sued the Topeka Board of Education, claiming that it was unconstitutional to make blacks attend separate schools from whites, most people thought that was a frivolous lawsuit. When Mrs. Liebeck sued McDonalds as a result of burns she received from McDonald's coffee, most people thought that was a frivolous lawsuit. They were wrong on both counts. Remember, a lawsuit is not frivolous just because somebody lost. Somebody loses in every lawsuit. Many lawsuits that started out being called frivolous have resulted in numerous changes for the good in our society.

Foreseeability test – A part of proving a claim for malpractice or negligence, the foreseeability test is an inquiry into whether the damages the plaintiff is claiming are foreseeable from the act of negligence the plaintiff is claiming. This is seldom a problem in professional negligence cases. Is it, for example, foreseeable that a lawyer's failure to file a lawsuit on time will result in dismissal of the lawsuit? Of course it is.

General partner – General partner can be used in two very different contexts and it is important to know which is being used. That phrase is sometimes used to designate someone who is a partner in a general partnership, which means that all of the partners are all equally liable for the debts and obligations of the partnership. Keep that in mind and pick your partners well before you enter into a general partnership. The term is also used, however, to designate that person or entity that is in charge of the affairs of a limited partnership. Limited partnerships have limited partners, who have no say in the operation of the partnership and no liability for partnership debts, but also have a "general partner" who is in charge of all of the management of the limited partnership and is also liable for all of the debts of the limited partnership.

Hedge fund – This term almost defies description today. Formally, a hedge fund was an investment vehicle to protect against an unforeseen decline in one investment in the future by and offsetting investment. If, for example, your business requires you to play roulette and you have five chips on black. You run the risk of losing all 5 chips. You could create your own "hedge fund" by placing two or three chips on red, thereby guaranteeing you will not lose all five chips. Today, however, hedge funds are high risk investment funds for the very wealthy who try to exploit or manipulate the stock market.

Initial public offering – Often referred by the shorthand of "IPO," an initial public offering is an offering of stock made from the company to the public. It is one of the ways companies raise more cash. By offering more stock to the public for sale, as distinguished from buying stock on the exchange through your broker, where you are simply purchasing the stock some other investor is selling but the company gets none of that money.

Interrogatories – One of several forms of "discovery" permitted by the courts, interrogatories are a series of questions in written form sent to the other side which the other side is required to answer within 30 days, typically. Failure to answer can result in sanctions by the court.

Investment advisor – Any one of several job titles of people who advise investors on the use of their money. Registered investment advisors recommend certain stock or bond purchases, although stockbrokers actually make the buys.

Investment portfolio – This term generally describes the overall look of your investments. You have a certain percent in equities, with shares in five or ten companies and a certain percent in bonds. Your investment portfolio might also include annuities or real estate holdings.

Judge – This is the person who presides over the trial and the appeal. Some judges are appointed for life, such as in the federal system, and some judges are elected and campaign much like other politicians, as state court judges in Texas do.

Jury – A group of private citizens numbering from six to 12 who become officers of the court and resolve factual disputes in lawsuits. More than any other county in the world, the United States trusts its citizens to assist the government in determining the guilt and innocence and the punishment of the people accused of crimes as well as the winners and losers in civil disputes. Jury duty is the most intimate interaction any citizen ever has with his or her government, unless he or she becomes an elected official.

Jury, grand – The grand jury is a part of the criminal justice system and, as initially intended, was to screen the government's indictment of its citizens by forcing the government to present the evidence against an individual before that person was forced to endure the expense and humiliation of a trial. It was based upon the premise that members of the grand jury would probably know the person and could make a credibility determination of witnesses and the accused, thereby ensuring that the government did not abuse its power by indicting people who did not deserve it. Today, however, the grand jury is routinely used as a tool of the government and more accurately resembles the inquisitor's courts of the inquisition than it does the original grand jury envisioned by our forefathers.

Kitchen table approach – This is the most elementary type of settlement negotiations, in which the two parties calmly sit down and work out disputes between themselves. This is especially used in family law.

Law clerks – These are usually law students or recent graduates from law school who for a year or two have accepted a job to assist the judge with legal research so that the judge's decisions can be well grounded in law. With a number of cases before them, most judges do not have the time to do independent research without law clerks.

Legal ethics – Lawyers are governed by a code of professional responsibility. The model code of ethics for lawyers was adopted by the American Bar Association (the "ABA") and has been adopted in most states, although changes on a state-by-state basis are not uncommon. The model rules are available on the ABA Web site and most states have their individual rules available on a Web site as well.

Legal cannibalism – Many people think this term simply refers to lawyers suing lawyers, which is what I do for a living. Cannibalism, however, requires something more than simply holding the profession accountable, which is what I think I do. When lawyers go after each other to settle a grudge or punish an adversary, when lawyers sue other lawyers simply because their own areas of expertise have dried up, that is what I call legal cannibalism.

Legal malpractice – Malpractice is just another word for negligence. When you run a red light, you're committing "driving malpractice." Legal malpractice consists of the same four elements as any other negligence based claim, all four elements described herein, which are duty, breach of duty, proximate cause, and damages.

Liability – In law school, we were taught that every trial consists of two phases, the liability and the damages phase. The liability phase concerns all of the evidence arguments and legal authorities that help determine whether one party owes money to another party, and the damage phase determines how much money is owed.

Limited partnership – A limited partnership is a legal entity where one group of partners (the limited partners) put up money but have no control over the partnership and no say in how it is run and no liability for the debts or obligations of the partnership. Every limited partnership must have one "general partner" who runs the affairs of the partnership and is liable for all of its debts. Limited partnerships are a common form of business entity in real estate investments and are becoming increasingly common with estate planners who set up family limited partnerships.

Liquid assets – Anything you own that is in cash or can be converted readily to cash. Stock in a publicly traded company is, for example, a liquid asset because it can be sold on the stock exchange and converted to cash within a matter of days. Real estate, however, is not a liquid asset because it cannot be sold as quickly and converted to cash.

Mail fraud – A federal crime which consists of committing an act of fraud through the use or instrumentality of the U.S. mail.

Mediation – A form of ADR in which the parties come together and use the help of a third party (the mediator) to try to resolve their differences. Until the 1980's, mediation was reserved almost exclusively for labor disputes, where a federal mediator would try to help unions and important industries such as the railroad or the trucking industry reach agreement on a collective bargaining agreement. Today, mediation is extremely common and it is almost impossible to get to trial without first having gone through the mediation process.

Medical board – Every state has an organization charged with overseeing the licensing of doctors in the state and to hear complaints against doctors. Complaints against doctors are sent to the board, but most citizens have found that the complaints simply go into a black hole and nothing ever happens to the doctor.

Medical Injury Compensation Reform Act of 1975 (MICRA) – This piece of legislation was passed in California and serves as a model for capping medical malpractice awards in various states.

Medical malpractice – Medical malpractice is simply negligence by a healthcare provider and consists of the same four elements as legal malpractice and negligence: duty, breach of the duty, proximate cause, and damages.

Money laundering – This is the process of taking "dirty money" and making it look clean. The dirty money could be the result of illegal activity, such as the sale of drugs or the sale of fraudulent securities. The cleaning process usually consists of funneling the money through some quasi-legitimate business.

Motion practice – Before any civil case gets to trial, the lawyers will have engaged in the motion practice which consists of efforts by the lawyers to refine and narrow the scope of the dispute. It may include a motion to limit the testimony of an expert witness or to prevent the other side from mentioning at trial certain irrelevant and highly prejudicial facts.

Mutual funds – These are amounts of money from various individuals and institutional investors that are used to purchase a diverse sampling of equities. In this way, investors purchase a wide variety of stocks and/ or bonds for a single fund and this is considered a far more diverse type of investment.

NASDAQ – The stock exchange in which trading takes place in most technology and new media stocks.

Non-economic damages – In most cases, this is called pain and suffering. The verdicts and settlements in most tort cases are a combination of economic and non-economic damages. Economic damages are the amount of money the injured person would have made during the time of the injury. Non-economic damages place a money amount on the pain and suffering of the victim, loss of companionship by a loved one because of injury or death, etc.

Pension plan – For decades, American workers were employed by a single company and benefitted from company pension plans which promised to pay them a set amount of money for life after they ended their employment.

Personal injury – This term relates to civil cases that involve injury to persons, including products liability, premises liability and professional malpractice.

Plaintiff – The person who files a civil law case.

Ponzi scheme – This scheme involves paying large returns on investments from the proceeds of subsequent investors rather than the creation of any real business. The original scheme, perpetrated by Charles Ponzi, was designed to exploit differing values for mail coupons. Ponzi's promise of extraordinary returns to the initial investors was paid by the money coming from later investors. Ponzi never actually bought any of the coupons on which the scheme was based.

Power of attorney – This is the power to sign agreements and make other legal moves for a person. Usually, someone gets power of attorney when a relative or loved one is incapacitated.

Preponderance of the evidence – This is the least stringent burden of proof in a civil case, meaning that more than 50% of the evidence is in favor of one party or the other. This is a much less strenuous standard than clear and convincing evidence or the criminal standard of the beyond a reasonable doubt.

Price/earnings ratio – The measure of the value of a stock is the price of a share divided into the annual earnings of the company.

Prospectus – The written material given to prospective buyers of stocks or bonds to give them an idea of the worthiness of the purchase.

Proximate cause – The most important element in a legal malpractice case, it consists of a two-part test. One part is the "foreseeability" test, meaning was the outcome foreseeable based on the actions of the attorney. The second part is the "but for" test – but for the actions of the attorney, would the bad outcome have happened?

Pyramid scheme – This is a scheme that involves soliciting investments, paying the first investors the promised return, then encouraging even more investors into the scheme. Eventually, you run out of money before you pay off investors. A Ponzi scheme is a type of pyramid scheme.

Recession – A sharp downturn in the economy consisting of at least two quarters of negative economic activity.

Referral agreement – An agreement for one attorney to refer a client to another attorney in exchange for some financial consideration, if the law of the jurisdiction allows.

Regulation T – This is a federal regulation pursuant to the authority of the Securities and Exchange Act of 1934 which changed the public's ability to buy stock with borrowed money. Reg T mandates that the customer can borrow no more than 50% of the value of the stock. If the value of the stock falls and, as a result, the customer's loan exceeds 50%, the broker may sell enough stock to lower the debt back to 50% of the value of the stock, without the customer's permission or consent.

Request for production – A form of discovery in which a party may require the opposing party to produce documents and tangible items deemed necessary to prove a civil case.

Request for admissions – A form of discovery in which one side asks the other to admit certain facts not in dispute so the parties do not have to take the time in the courtroom on matters they agree upon.

Restitution – A measure of damages often used in fraud or contract cases in which a party seeks to be put in the position they were in prior to the fraud or breach of contract.

Return on investment (ROI) – This is a comparison of how much money the investment will cost versus how much money you will make from the investment. Usually expressed as a percentage, ROI tells you how long you will have to hold an investment before you make your money back. A red flag for many investments is the promises of an extraordinary high ROI.

Sanctions – Any kind of penalty accessed by a court or arbitrator based upon someone's violation or abuse of the rules governing the conduct in a trial or arbitration proceeding.

Settlement – The most common outcome of a civil law case. Up to 90% of all cases settle through informal attorney-to-attorney negotiations or more formal avenues such as mediation or arbitration.

Stockbroker fraud – This is a catch-all term for the many ways a person can be victimized by a stockbroker or other investment advisor.

Statute of limitations – The amount of time that the law allows after the commission of a bad act for the victim of that act to file a lawsuit.

Supreme Court – Usually the highest court in a state or the nation, although some trial courts in New York State are called supreme courts. These highest courts usually only hear appeals of cases with a wide application of the law.

Tax shelter – Vehicles created by intentional or unintentional loopholes in tax law that allow taxpayers to exempt certain investments from taxation.

Torts – Tort law is the name given to a body of law that creates, and provides remedies for, civil wrongs that do not arise out of contractual duties.

Tort reform – The movement to restrict the application of tort law and caps damages for violation of those laws.

Transactional lawyer – An attorney whose forte is writing contracts, setting up corporations, and generally overseeing and advising on business transactions. Unlike litigators, transactional lawyers, rarely if ever go to court (except as a defendant in a malpractice case).

Transparency – The ability to see exactly how a situation works. Once a pejorative, transparency is now considered a good thing. Only invest when you can see exactly where the money is going, how it will be used and how you can recover your investment.

U.S. Pension Benefit Guaranty Corporation – The government corporation that guarantees the payment of pension benefits.

Unsuitability – An advisor who owes a fiduciary duty to a client is required to invest his or her money only in situations that suit the client's circumstances. For instance, if the client wants only to protect the principle and have ready access to the money, investment in a highly speculative real estate venture where the money would be tied up for years would not be suitable.

Wealth management – A fancy name for the work of a financial planner or investment advisor who restricts his or her work to people with a minimum amount of money to invest.

White collar crime – Another term for robbery at pen point. White collar criminals are "the Suits" who steal your money through professional means.

Venue – This is the decision of the jury at the conclusion of a trial. Once the jury returns its verdict, the court then will be asked to reduce that verdict to a final judgment of the court.

Verdict – The result of a trial, issued either by a judge or a jury. Most cases end by settlement, but those that go the court end in a verdict for one side or the other.

Notes

Front Matter and Prologue

1. This quote comes from Woody Guthrie's *Pretty Boy Floyd*, circa 1958.

2. My feeling about Audie Murphy comes from memories of that young kid in the cowboy costume. The details of Murphy's short life and demise came from www.arlingtoncemetery.org.

Chapter 1

1. I appropriated the story of author Joseph Heller, Kurt Vonnegut and the hedge fund manager at a cocktail party from an address by John Bogle, the founder of Vanguard Investments, on the occasion of his acceptance of an honorary doctor of humane letters degree before MBA graduates of the McDonough School of Business at Georgetown University, May 18, 2007.

2. Jeffrey Skilling's tribulations were taken from the Rochester, Minnesota *Post-Bulletin*, December 21, 2006, and *Texas Lawyer*, April 7, 2008.

Chapter 2

1. The story of John Anthony Williams' defrauding of Loyd Stubbs was taken from a press release issued April 16, 2004 by the U.S. Attorney's Office for the District of Oregon, and from various news accounts from the area.

2. The account of lawyer James W. Brill's participation in the defrauding of Loyd Stubbs was taken primarily from Case No. 05-82, Order Approving Stipulation for Discipline, the Supreme Court of the State of Oregon, dated May 15, 2006.

3. Income statistics under the subhead, "We Worship the Gods and Goddesses of Success," come from various reports prepared by the U.S. Census Bureau, an agency of the U.S. Department of Labor.

4. The story about George W. Bush allowing school districts to misuse state funds was related to me by my publisher.

5. The editorial on oversight of the mortgage crisis is excerpted from "Not Much of a Watchdog," *The New York Times*, April, 17, 2008.

6. The story of the Michael Pickens pump and dump scheme was taken from a press release originating from the U.S. Attorney's Office for the Southern District of New York, October 30, 2006; and from various news accounts.

7. Texas Senator John Cornyn's attack on the courts and judges was taken from "Senator Links Violence to 'Political' Decisions," *The Washington Post*, April 5, 2005.

8. The American Bar Association's film and companion materials under the heading of "Countering the Critics," were prepared by Margie Elsberg of Elsberg Associates for the Least Understood Branch group, a joint project of the American Bar Association Judicial Division and Standing Committee on Judicial Independence, 2006.

9. The discussion of caps on malpractice lawsuits came from the "Weiss Ratings: Medical Malpractice Caps – The Impact of Non-economic Damage Caps," June 2, 2003.

10. The quote from Texas Trial Lawyers Association President Paul Waldner is from "Texas' tort reform," *The Oklahoma City Journal Record*, April 18, 2008.

11. I adapted the story of the McDonald's hot coffee lawsuit from the publication *Voir Dire*, Fall-Winter, 2007.

Chapter 3

1. Information on the effects of malpractice caps was taken from "Hurt? Injured? Need a Lawyer? Too Bad!," *Texas Monthly*, November 2005.

2. The rise of creative legal thinking was chronicled in "The Legacy of the Warren Court," *TIME* magazine, July 4, 1969.

3. Information on Sarbanes-Oxley and the comments of Michael Oxley were taken from "Sarbanes-Oxley doing its job, co-author says," *Honolulu Star-Bulletin*, December 2, 2007.

4. Statistics on taxation in the U.S. were taken from the book, *10 Excellent Reasons Not to Hate Taxes*, The New Press, 2007.

Chapter 4

1. Most of the information in this section about how I started in malpractice was taken from a speech I give to both business and

professional groups, titled "Why I Sue Lawyers." The speech, which can be accessed on my law firm's website, www.johnstontobey.com, was originally written for a meeting of insurance industry executives.

2. The interview with Michael Quinn, an adjunct professor at the University of Texas School of Law, was conducted by telephone on March 26, 2007.

3. Details of the Ventas lawsuit against the law firm of Sullivan & Cromwell came from "Lawyer vs. Lawyer Becoming Common Corporate Strategy," *Chicago Tribune* Business section, February 12, 2006. We also used various Internet news accounts, such as a release on www.lawyersandsettlements.com and www.mcknights.com.

4. Statistics on the number of legal malpractice cases were taken from *The Advocate*, a publication of The Bar Plan Mutual Insurance Company, Winter 2006. Much of the information in this article came from Profile of Legal Malpractice Claims 2000-2003 by the American Bar Association's Standing Committee on Lawyers' Professional Liability.

Chapter 5

1. The JP Morgan quote when asked what the market will do, "It will fluctuate," is from www.memorable-quotes.com.

2. The information on Regulation T was taken from various web accounts and histories provided by the Securities and Exchange Commission.

Information on the growth of investing comes from the article, "Americans Bank on Stocks; Nearly 50% of Households Put Faith in Market," *The Washington Post*, October 22, 1999.

3. The story of MP3.com's rise and fall came from two sources: "MP3.com an Example of Wall Street Shortsightedness," *Los Angeles Business Journal*, August 2, 1999; "Going Public With MP3.com," *Internet World*, June 7, 1999.

4. The information on Dennis Herula came from the *Rocky Mountain News*, February 12, 2005.

5. Descriptions of the various job descriptions in investment circles came from the website of the SEC.

Chapter 6

1. The interview with plaintiff's personal injury attorney Paula Sweeney was done by telephone on February 1, 2007.

2. The startling revelations about the number of deaths in American hospitals came from the 2006 report of the Institutes of Medicine of The National Academies.

3. When actor Dennis Quaid's two babies were the victims of medical errors, there were many news accounts of the near-tragedy. His appearance before Congress was chronicled on the CBS newsmagazine, *60 Minutes*, on May 14, 2008.

4. The story of the Medical Injury Compensation Reform Act of 1975

(MICRA) came from a report titled "Medical Liability Reform – Now!," a compendium of facts supporting medical liability reform and debunking arguments against reform, American Medical Association, July 19, 2006.

Chapter 7

1. The story of C.L. Nathanson's difficulty with her business partners came from the case I handled for her in the mid-1990s. I refreshed my memory about the details with a series of telephone interviews in May 2008.

2. Wal-Mart's tax avoidance schemes are chronicled by the website *Wal-Mart Watch*, in a report dated March 2007 and revised in October 2007. I supplemented this information from reports on several blogs, including *The Daily Kos*, from this same time period.

Chapter 8

1. The sad story of my ill-fated investment in Zee Best comes from a part of my history of which I am not particularly proud. To refresh my memory on the details of ZZZ Best and its wunderkind owner, Barry Minkow, I consulted a number of web accounts of his rise, fall and present circumstances as a crusader against people like himself.

2. The outrageous story of scammer Reed Slatkin first came to my attention from the syndicated television show, *American Greed*, in 2007.

3. Linda Eads, associate professor of law at the Southern Methodist

University Dedman School of Law, spoke to us by telephone on February 20, 2007. Her insight into the behavior of people who rob at pen point validated our experience with those people.

4. The Nigerian email scam came to the inbox of my publisher, Larry Upshaw, on September 10, 2008. This was an email warning from AARP.

5. The more refined version of the email scam, in which the dishonest person addresses the recipient by name, came to the inbox of Upshaw's son, Corbin.

6. Ponzi schemes are a fairly common method of scamming people, and they are especially useful against the more sophisticated investor. So we have seen Ponzi schemes in action before. In most cases, we are skeptical about information gleaned from the Internet, but we consulted numerous Internet sources to learn about Charles Ponzi.

7. Gregory Setser – The tale of the Ponzi scheme he and his sister used to defraud evangelical Christians of more than $170 million first appeared in "Jury Convicts Brother, Sister of Swindling Church Members," *The Dallas Morning News*, June 13, 2006.

8. This list of guidelines for protecting yourself from pen point thievery was excerpted from the website of the Securities and Exchange Commission.

9. The three examples of scams that have a tinge of authenticity to them were constructed from fact patterns of various cases my firm has handled over the years.

Chapter 10

1. As stated in the text, Howard Byrnes was a client of ours. We handled his case against the attorney Charles Bundren. We confirmed the details of this story with Howard in a telephone interview on February 1, 2008.

2. Our interview with Fred Moss, associate professor at the Southern Methodist University Dedman School of Law, on the subject of legal ethics and the duty owed from the attorney to the client, took place by telephone on February 5, 2007.

3. Information on fee arrangements and the relationship of the attorney to his or her client come from our practice and conversations with several other attorneys who offer contingent fee arrangements.

Chapter 11

1. We interviewed Daniel B. Moisand, a wealth manager in Melbourne, Florida, by telephone on January 22, 2007.

2. Information about the certified financial planner (CFP) designation and the duties of those who have this certification were taken from documents from The Financial Planning Association, the North American Securities Administrators Association (NASAA) and the SEC's investment advisor public disclosure web site.

3. The idea for the couch potato approach to investing originated with Scott Burns, who at the time was personal finance columnist for *The Dallas Morning News*. His article, "Exactly How to Be A Couch Potato

Portfolio Manager," first appeared in *The News* business section on October 1, 1991. I used this article plus a followup story, "Personal Finance Writer Scott Burns Applies, Extends Famed 'Couch Potato Investing...' that ran on the *Business Wire,* February 20, 2008.

Chapter 12

1. Dr. D. Larry Crumbley at LSU is a very different individual – an inventive and colorful accountant. The quote from him at the beginning of this chapter is from "LSU forensic accounting and internal audit course prepare students for hot careers," *LSU Highlights,* September 10, 2008.

2. The interview with Ken Travis at Travis Wolff & Associates took place February 12, 2007 and was by telephone.

Chapter 13

1. My publisher, Larry Upshaw, related this story of his dealings with a cardiac surgeon. The incident took place in 1992. Upshaw, age 45, has a family history of heart disease. For him, the decision to rebuff the original surgeon put forth by the hospital was a good one. While he remains under a doctor's care, Upshaw is living a good life in his sixties.

2. The information on physician-owned hospitals comes from "Should Doctors Own Hospitals?," *BusinessWeek,* February 20, 2006.

Chapter 14

1. The quote about how lawyer advertising has helped to spawn lawyer jokes is taken from an article in the *Georgetown Journal of Legal Ethics*, Summer 2005.

2. For the section, Marketing in the Internet Era, I simply googled "Family Law Attorney Denver."

3. *Law and Politics Media* runs two campaigns each year in Texas, as in most other states. They select Texas Super Lawyers and Texas Rising Stars. Much of the information in this section was taken from informal conversations (I hesitate to call them interviews) with people from *Law and Politics Media* by my publisher.

Chapter 15

1. Medical apology programs were described in "Physician's News Digest," February 2005, and "Impact of Medical Apology Statutes and Policies," *Journal of Nursing Law*, April 1, 2008.

2. A story in *The Washington Post*, "Medical Boards Let Physicians Practice Despite Drug Abuse," April 10, 2005, tells about doctors with drug problems being allowed to continue practicing.

3. The queen of home organization, Kathy Beauchamp, spoke to us about how good organization contributes to any case you might have against a professional in a telephone interview on June 15, 2008.

Chapter 18

1. The conversation we had with mediator and arbitrator Will Pryor took place by telephone March 27, 2007.

Chapter 19

1. The quote from family lawyer Kevin Fuller was excerpted and adapted with permission from the chapter on collaborative law in the book, *Lone Star Divorce*, 2008.

2. This study on the value of settling a case rather than going to court first appeared in the *Journal of Empirical Legal Studies*. The article that was the basis of this sidebar, "Study Finds Settling Is Better Than Going to Trial," came from *The New York Times*, August 8, 2008.

Chapter 20

1. Details of the Gateway computer cases going to arbitration were taken from "Arbitration Trend Fuels Consumer Lawsuits; Binding Terms Added to Contracts," *Chicago Tribune*, May 30, 2004.

Chapter 21

1. I coined the term "Legal Cannibalism." Details of the Jamail-O'Quinn rivalry was taken from the article, "Legal trend of leveling suits against fellow litigators likened to cannibalism," *The Houston Chronicle*, July 21, 2007.

Chapter 22

1. The story of criminal activities at the law firm of Milberg Weiss Bershad Hynes & Lerach was adapted from the article, "Big Penalty Set for Law Firm, But Not a Trial," *The New York Times*, June 17, 2008.

2. The interview of criminal defense attorney Ted Steinke was done by telephone on February 27, 2007.

3. Statistics on concentrated wealth comes from "New Data Show Extraordinary Jump In Income Concentration in 2004," *Center on Budget and Policy Priorities*, October 13, 2006.

4. Statistics on the transfer of wealth from The Greatest Generation to the Baby Boomers comes from "Baby Boomer Wealth Transfer," *Insurance Journal*, February 23, 2004.

5. The story of the fight for control of the Pritzker fortune comes from "Pritzker v. Pritzker," *Forbes* magazine, November 24, 2003.

6. The interview of Kathy Muldoon, vice president of Carter Financial Management, took place by telephone on March 22, 207.

7. The story of the money dispute within the family of Mary Kay Ash comes from "Mary Kay heirs at odds over trust funds," *The Dallas Morning News*, November 6, 2006.

Randy Johnson is managing partner of the Dallas-based professional malpractice law firm of Johnston Tobey, P.C. He is a passionate and knowledgeable speaker and writer on the subject of preventing people from being robbed at pen point.

Randy is available to speak to civic and professional groups on this subject throughout the country. He can be reached at 214 741-6260 or by email at coytrandal@johnstontobey.com.

Groups wishing to purchase copies of this book by the carton at discount prices can do so at www.psgbooks.com.